Jun. 2013

BETTER HOMES AND GARDENS®

Makeovers
room-by-room solutions

A **Better Homes and Gardens**. Book
An Imprint of

HMH

Published by:
Houghton Mifflin Harcourt
Boston • New York
www.hmhbooks.com

For information about permission to reproduce selections from this book, write to Permissions, Houghton Mifflin Harcourt Publishing Company, 215 Park Avenue South, New York, New York 10003.

www.hmhbooks.com

Library of Congress Control Number available from the publisher upon request.
ISBN: 978-1-118-38864-8 (pbk)

Printed in the United States of America

DOR 10 9 8 7 6 5 4 3 2 1

BETTER HOMES AND GARDENS® MAGAZINE
Gayle Goodson Butler
Executive Vice President, Editor in Chief
Oma Blaise Ford
Executive Editor
Mike Belknap
Creative Director

BETTER HOMES AND GARDENS® MAKEOVERS
Editor: Paula Marshall
Contributing Editors: Jean Schissel Norman and Meredith Ladik
Contributing Designer: Kristin Cleveland
Contributing Copy Editor: Angela K. Renkoski
Contributing Photographer: Marty Baldwin
Contributing Producer: Katie Leporte
Cover Photographer: Kim Cornelison

SPECIAL INTEREST MEDIA
Editorial Director: James Blume
Content Core Director, Home: Jill Waage
Deputy Content Core Director, Home: Karman Hotchkiss
Managing Editor: Doug Kouma
Art Director: Gene Rauch
Group Editor: Lacey Howard
Copy Chief: Jennifer Speer Ramundt
Business Director: Janice Croat

MEREDITH NATIONAL MEDIA GROUP
President: Tom Harty
Executive Vice President: Doug Olson

MEREDITH CORPORATION
President and Chief Executive Officer: Stephen M. Lacy

HOUGHTON MIFFLIN HARCOURT
Vice President and Publisher: Natalie Chapman
Editorial Director: Cindy Kitchel
Acquisitions Editor: Pam Mourouzis
Production Director: Diana Cisek
Production Manager: John Simko

Time for a new look

From redoing a bookcase to refreshing a room, you'll find inspiration and advice here.

Whatever the scope of your makeover, this book is for you. To start your projects, large and small, check out the ideas and advice in "Getting Started" (page 6). Keep the makeover momentum going with the amazing real-life before-and-after examples in "Room by Room" (page 14). When you're ready to transform your whole house, "House Tours" (page 122) will be your guide. Everyone can use a little help with the hands-on details: In "Make It Yours" (page 148), follow step-by-step instructions to create fabulous new pieces from found treasures or items you already own. Enjoy your makeover!

contents

SECTION ONE
room by room

SECTION TWO
house tours

SECTION THREE
make it yours

also in this book

a fresh look | *expert advice*

A makeover is as much a mind-set as a process. Here are some idea starters from a few of our favorite designers and writers.

"Just collecting images isn't enough. When I save a picture, I note the specific things that drew my attention. Let the details you love be a compass to guide your makeovers—from a single item to a whole house."

—**Steve Fuller,** blogger, *anurbancottage.blogspot.com*

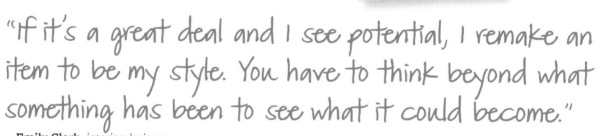

before

"If it's a great deal and I see potential, I remake an item to be my style. You have to think beyond what something has been to see what it could become."

—**Emily Clark,** interior designer

"Paint + masking tape + imagination lets me play with straight lines and fun color combinations for walls, floors, and furniture."

—**Jean Norman,** writer and designer

"Look at shape more than finish when you're shopping. Dated wood grain disappears with a coat of paint, but gorgeous lines last forever."

—**Shannon Kaye,** interior designer

"THINK OF A LAMP AND ITS SHADE AS SEPARATES, JUST LIKE A BLAZER AND SLACKS. CHANGE THE SHADE, AND YOU HAVE A WHOLE NEW LOOK."

—**Elain Griffith,** interior designer

"If an item is designed to go on the floor, pick it up and put it anywhere but. A great throw rug can make a great table or sideboard cover—in some cases, even a wall hanging."

—**Kathleen Hackett,** author of *Home from the Hardware Store*

Makeover must-haves

When the urge strikes to redo a table, a room, or a house, be prepared to jump right in. Here is a starter list of items to have on hand.

Toolbox
Have the basic tools at the ready: tape measure, flat and Phillips screwdrivers, pliers, hammer, level, picture-hanging kit, and a notepad with pencil or a notes app on your phone.

Paint kit
Since paint is a makeover maven's best friend, having the hardware ready means all you need is the paint. The basics for your kit are a sash brush, large and small roller frames and covers, paint trays and liners, a drop cloth, and painter's tape.

Apps and online tools
Bookmark the pages and download apps that best serve you. Register for My Color Finder on *BHG.com* for hue help for any project. Also on the site are how-to videos and tons of DIY advice.

Idea file
Nothing beats file folders or notebooks for collecting magazine pages; *Pinterest.com* is great for flagging and sorting ideas online. Spend a few pleasant hours sorting your lists at least once a year. Not only will the exercise inspire you, it will keep your best ideas from getting buried with the outdated ones.

50 ideas to try today

Rethink. Re-imagine. Redo.
Change starts right here. Enjoy!

1 Tie a silk scarf around a pillow for an instant refresher.

2 Create a bouquet by massing mini vases holding one rose each.

3. Collect unused items from each room; donate or sell.

4. Gather objects by color or shape; display together for impact.

5. Swap your linens. Combine pillowcases from one set with sheets from another.

6. Use a classic chair as an easel-style display for artwork.

7 Bring in nature—stones, shells, or pinecones—to fill a pedestal bowl.

8. Gather items in your favorite colors. Store them in a basket until you're ready to redecorate.

9 Use trays to display objects on a coffee table, gather gear on a nightstand, or corral cell phones and coins on an entry table.

10. Tuck a prized family snapshot into the frame of a fancy hallway mirror.

11. Make a temporary end table by stacking oversize art and design books next to a cherished chair.

12. Clear out accessories room by room. For a fresh look, bring them back one by one, leaving some in storage.

13. Enlarge a child's drawing; frame it for display.

14 Start building a color palette by tagging favorite hues.

15 Fill pretty bowls with everyday items, such as twine balls or loose change.

16. Display jewelry on a bedroom dresser in a way that's handy yet personal.

Group likes with likes—arrange books by color, gather white objects for the mantel, or fill a storage cabinet with identical containers.

18 Shake things up. Reconsider furniture and accessory pairings, and rearrange and experiment with new options.

19 Use stacked books to create artsy display pedestals on any surface.

20. Toss a throw over the back of a chair for a color lift.

21. Hang a metal tray on the wall; use magnets to turn it into a memo or message board.

22. Put a catchall basket near the front door to hide clutter.

23. Place a small basket or box on the coffee table to conceal the remote.

24. Hang a large mirror above the fireplace for a dramatic look.

25. Perk up storage containers with pretty labels; purchase them or make them yourself. (*Download a stash of free labels at* **BHG.com/makeoverlabels.**)

26 Stand a pretty platter behind a faucet as an instant splashguard.

27. Unroll a bold striped rug to add color and pattern to a neutral kitchen.

Hang a large piece of art off-center above a dresser or sofa.

33. Perk up a nightstand with fresh flowers.

29. Cast a new light by changing the shades on lamps in the living room.

30. Hang mirrors on a wall opposite windows to maximize natural light.

31. Rearrange books and add artwork to shelves.

32. Swap items from room to room—move a side chair to the bedroom, for example—to give both the spaces and the pieces a fresh new look.

34

Prop decoratively framed mirrors on a sideboard.

35. Dip an artist's brush into a pot of paint and dab it on a simple frame. Instant color!

50 ideas to try today

36 Spray-paint a lamp base a bold, fresh hue.

37. Place a lamp on the kitchen countertop for instant mood lighting.

38. Reconsider texture pairings: rattan with silver, stone with crystal, or silk with burlap.

39. Replace just the pillow shams to freshen a bed.

40. Add pattern and color by lining the inside of an open cabinet with wrapping paper.

41. Lean a framed print on the windowsill to minimize a bad view.

42. Add height and drama by cutting a tall sapling and "planting" it in a weighted container.

Slip a single elegant leaf into a clear glass cylinder.

43

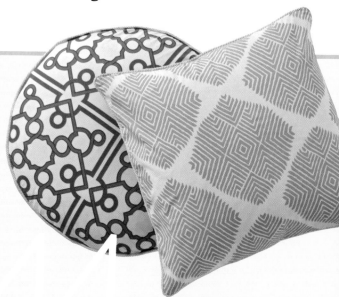

Toss a new pillow onto a favorite chair.

45. Rotate the sofa toward an inspiring view.

46. Fill mugs or short vases with spoons, forks, and knives for a pretty grab-and-go flatware sorter.

47. Use a metallic paint pen to add a little gleam to the edges of a worn metal light fixture.

48. Freshen chairs with paint in coordinating colors on all or part of each leg.

49 Create a pot rack by hanging a sturdy branch above an island. Suspend items from S hooks.

50 Set the table with a combo of old and new dishes in a mix of colors and patterns.

room by room

Life unfolds in every room at home, so why settle for ho-hum? Let us help with design tips and secrets that show you how to uncover and express your personal style.

living rooms

Your style changes, and so should your living room's look.
Be fearless; revamp the room so it best reflects what you love.

Time for Change. IN AN HOUR.

Move the sofa to take in the best view: a wall of windows in summer and the fireplace in winter. Change what's resting on the mantel to reflect the season too: Add garden-picked leaves and blooms in clear glass vases in the summer. In cooler seasons, display an array of shapely twigs or a bowl of pinecones or acorns. Add or delete color for instant dramatic change: Swap a patterned rug for plain sisal to inject comfort and personality. Or toss a colorful throw over a neutral upholstered chair for a quick makeover. **IN AN AFTERNOON.** Raise the perceived ceiling height by hanging curtains and blinds a few inches below the ceiling. Make a small window seem more grand by installing curtain panels to hang just beyond the window on both sides. Rethink the furniture arrangement to suit how you plan to use the room. Do you need a reading corner? Room for a writing desk? Space for toys? Slip furniture sliders under major pieces to make light work of moving. **IN A WEEKEND.** Redo the wall above the sofa by "shopping" in your house for favorite pieces of art. Start with a central dominant framed piece and surround it with smaller pieces in a variety of shapes, sizes, and formats. Paint the ceiling an inspiring color, such as pale violet to lift gray walls or soft blue to give the feeling of endless sky.

before & after | color play

This ordinary room became a style star and conquered the blahs with smart color choices. Small changes added up to a big masterpiece.

before

COLOR BLOCK

left Every room needs a bit of contrasting color for visual success. The green chairs, bright throw pillows, raspberry lamp bases and ottoman, and teal chair create a horizontal swath of complementary color against the neutral sofa and carpet.

KICK IT UP

below left A trio of kicky yellow bookcases opposite the sofa lend balance and interest. Although they fill the wall, they actually make the wall seem bigger. Bold accents, such as the orbs on the middle shelf, work like jewelry to add personality and pizzazz to the room.

before

HANG ART
Artwork doesn't have to be expensive to make a statement. Try this budget-savvy framing strategy: Use ready-made natural-wood frames and have mats custom-cut at least 3 inches wide. This strategy gives your walls the attitude of an art gallery.

refresh
Give a lamp a different look with a new shade in a new shape—wider or narrower, taller or shorter than the old shade.

before & after | *feather the nest*

Flat and drab gave way to color and pattern. Shades of sky, grass, and sun reflect nature's palette while bold prints feature modern botanicals.

refresh
Stacked mirrors expand the view, reflect light, and mimic windows.

before

OPEN UP

above **Moving the sofa to the window wall deemphasizes its presence and opens up the 12×21-foot room to a more welcoming arrangement. The fireplace wall becomes a focal point with a large print above the mantel that is a better scale for the space. Instead of one gigantic mirror, smaller, curvier alternatives flank the mantel.**

OPT FOR PATTERN

opposite **New drapes are the pattern star of the living room. They also camouflage small windows by extending 6 inches beyond the window frame on each side. The drapes' botanical fabric ties in with other nature-inspired elements, such as the branch-look lamps, ceramic garden stool, and framed artwork.**

try it | 6 great ideas

Whether your living room is a quiet and formal zone or an anything-goes space, make it work for how you live.

1 GO BOLD

Rich teal walls add instant warmth and make this small living room feel larger. Layers of light neutrals for the upholstery, rug, and accessories keep the mood airy. An upholstered ottoman doubles as a coffee table and footrest.

refresh

Fit a roll-up blind inside the window frame to save space and expose attractive millwork.

2 DRESS UP

above left **Formal yet friendly, this soothing living space mixes comfort with sparkle. Glass surfaces reflect light; wood finishes add warmth. The blue walls mimic sky while soft tan-gold on the crown molding echoes the room's gilded touches.**

3 GATHER ROUND

above right **Centering a seating area around a fireplace encourages conviviality. A neutral palette mixes with textures and patterns to create a look that's warm and inviting. And the zebra-print chair? That's a surprise element.**

4 SETTLE DOWN

right **An L-shape sectional and pairs of chairs and ottomans offer plenty of casual gathering space. The centered coffee table makes room for drinks, dinner, and board games. Pillows and throws add color and comfort.**

refresh
Hang a chandelier so the bottom gives you at least 6 feet 8 inches of head space from the floor.

5

Break a large room into activity areas. Place a table and chairs at one end for games and a sectional at the other end for media entertainment.

5 GET COLOR
above Classic architecture and traditional furniture mix it up with bold pops of yellow and mango to create a formal look that's livable and easygoing. Sink-in seating, plump pillows, and a thick rug supply comfort.

6 REST EASY
opposite Materials matter when it comes to casual style. Natural linen upholstery and pillows and metallic furniture and lighting fixtures deliver style with a relaxed—but not slouchy—air. Furniture with storage corrals the clutter.

refresh
An overhead
pendant
and sconces
offer lighting
flexibility.

style basics | *fireplaces*

The hearth has always been a gathering spot. Today's versions offer surprising material mixes and overscale charm.

<< ideas to steal

- A fireplace that's both tall and wide creates drama, while traditional woodwork details keep it homey in a classic house. The adjacent bookcase complements the visual weight of the fireplace.

- Bold and striking, the surround of large stones directs attention to the fire; painted woodwork and beaded-board insets above the mantel and on the ceiling play supporting roles.

- Simple furniture and accessories, edited for emphasis, effectively keep the spotlight on the hearth.

>> ideas to steal

- A stacked-stone fireplace establishes lodge style; stretching the stone to the ceiling adds visual heft that can make ceilings seem taller.

- Stone is the only star. Using it for every bit of fireplace real estate, including the hearth and mantel, adds to the impact. Look for real stone veneer products that deliver the look for less than hand-cut stone.

- Surround the fireplace with accessories that support the look: glass seltzer bottles, a crock for firewood, and a rusted metal star.

refresh
Gather firewood in a vintage crock, large basket, or copper pot.

color | *shades of life*

Stymied by color choices? Look here for how to translate a colorful find into the inspiration for living room decor.

refresh
Maintain the color mood with flowers in a single green hue.

Sherwin Williams
Kilkenny 6740

Benjamin Moore
Baby Turtle 515

GREEN WITH ENVY

left **Base a color scheme on a favorite fabric. These kelly green and white draperies inspired accessories in a range of greens. The neutral grass-cloth backdrop delivers a big lesson: Bold hues paired with warm neutrals yield sophistication.**

ARTFUL HUES
left A prized piece of art reflects your emotional connection to a color. Grab that choice and use it to transform a room. Here, soft blue on the walls echoes the vibrant blue of the framed artwork. Expand the palette with yellow, blue's complementary hue.

Valspar
Churchill Hotel Ivory 3007-8C

Sherwin Williams
Aquarium 6767

Sherwin Williams
Minor Blue 6792

refresh
Simplify collections and maintain open space on shelves.

Living room storage has to look good and work hard. Bookcases handle both requirements with style.

NICHE DESIGN
Handsome and utilitarian, this custom bookcase offers niches for art and books, and base cabinets that flip open. Look for off-the-rack versions you can adapt for your collections.

A library of books warms up a room and adds character.

READING CABINET

above left **Art, collections, and books find a home inside and on top of this freestanding cabinet. Select the bookcase color to contrast or to blend with the contents.**

WONDER WALL

above right **Shallow cabinets stretch from corner to corner and to the ceiling with hidden storage below and book display above. Add a contrasting color to the back of the bookcase to create a fun backdrop.**

ADDED VALUE

right **An attached table turns a bookcase into a home office, media center, and cabinet for reference materials and curios. Consider this arrangement for a narrow wall at one end of a long room.**

dining rooms

Take your dining room from stale to striking with our bite-size ideas for adding style, comfort, and function.

Time for Change. IN AN HOUR.

Scour your entertaining wares for fresh ideas for accessories such as an array of candlesticks or a single large serving dish to anchor the table's decor. Unfurl a graphic runner down the dining table's center, then parade along its length classic clay pots and glass jars filled with flowers, produce, or whatever catches your eye in the pantry or garden. Include votives at every setting for dining by candlelight. **IN AN AFTERNOON.** Dust off pretty plates hiding in your hutch and hang them above a sideboard. Paint a prim dining table a head-turning color or a cool, sophisticated metallic. Re-cover seats of side chairs in a new fabric; pick a stain-resistant outdoor fabric that cleans up easily. Resuscitate an aged brass chandelier with black paper shades, and adhere gold leaf to the inside of the shades for a wink of glamour. **IN A WEEKEND.** Adhere a peel-and-stick vinyl decal of a cherry blossom tree or other wall-size motif and get the drama of a mural without the hassle of installing or removing a real one. Browse artist e-commerce websites such as *etsy.com* for affordable, unique decals. Shop your other rooms for furniture: Relocate a comfy pair of living room armchairs to the dining table. Swap a picnic bench for side chairs. Or reassign a hall console table or bedroom dresser as a bar or buffet.

before & after | history class

This bare-bones room became a classic with vintage-style built-ins, homespun textiles, and subdued finishes.

refresh
Wallpaper the interior of a closet for the look of an old steamer trunk.

before

COZY COMFORT

above left **Built-in bookcases and a window seat pump up the volume of a wall. The result is cozy not cramped. The no-sew seat cushion is made from two lumbar pillows tucked into vintage laundry bags. Paint colors on the built-ins mimic the scheme of the linen-upholstered, leather-trimmed chairs.**

SNEAK EASY

above right **When space is at a premium, get creative—and covert—with storage. This coat closet moonlights as a bar created from old leather and wicker suitcases stacked atop an upholstered stool. A serving tray creates a level surface for bottles and glasses.**

DARKER SIDE

opposite **Burnished metals and dark wood tones give this room an aged look. Tarnished trophy-shape vases complement a bronze chandelier, and a walnut table links to displays of wood and metal boxes. Dark brown paint on the back of the built-ins ties into the scheme while keeping the look light and bright.**

refresh
A work of contemporary art offsets a room's traditional vibe.

before & after | *eye-opener*

before

Cavelike. Awkward. Unused. Sound familiar?
A good furniture arrangement and color will
entice your family back to the table.

SMART MOVE
above **Turn your
dining table sideways
and scoot it up to a
picture window to
free up floor space
and improve traffic
flow. Replace a formal
dining set with a
parson's table and
mismatched chairs
for a fresh look. Aqua
grass cloth was
attached to the back
of the shelves with
adhesive transfer
tape for an easy-to-
change hit of color.**

COLOR BOOST
left **Zippy modern
fabric patterns and a
Florida-sunshine
palette keep the room
from being staid.
Cushions with
tropical punch,
elegant Roman
shades, and wooden
recessed panels
update the built-in
window seat. The
upholstered pieces
and fluffy pillows
offer comfort.**

DUAL DUTY
opposite **This table
was built by screwing
2×4 legs into a
plywood top. Its skirt
was sewn from
indoor-outdoor
fabric. Ribbon-width
fusible webbing
makes adding
grosgrain trim a
breeze. Don't like a
mirror's color? Be
fearless. Spray-paint
it a different color
(or white). Ditto
with lamps.**

refresh
Slipcover a
console table,
then slide
a cabinet
underneath
for hidden
buffet storage.

Comfortable, casual seating in the dining room is the foundation of long-lasting family gatherings.

refresh
Attach an oversize black fabric shade to a pendant light kit to add drama to a small dining area.

1 TUCKED IN

opposite **A corner-hugging, built-in bench and side chairs maximize seating space—and the cozy quotient—in a snug dining room. Pull-out drawers beneath the bench provide bonus storage space.**

2 SLIP UP

above left **Slipcovers are a dining room's best friend. They instantly change a room's mood. Slip on white canvas covers to kick off the easy, breezy summer season; they pull off easily to toss in the wash when soiled. If you can't sew, search the Internet for ready-made versions and custom slipcover tailors.**

3 CHECKS BALANCE

above right **How do you begin a room makeover? Pick a fabric, such as the floral upholstery on this room's chairs, and repeat one or more of its colors in drapes, wall paint, and accessories. For balance, use a mix of pattern sizes, such as the oversize check and tight floral here.**

4 ROOM DIVIDER

right **Replicate the intimate ambience of a restaurant booth by sliding a high-back love seat up to a table. The settee also serves as a room divider, establishing a separate dining space within an open room. No building required.**

refresh
String garlands of wood balls connected by eye hooks through a classic iron chandelier for an eco-chic light.

5 CLEAR CONNECTION

opposite **Forget** peeling-paint furniture and frilly drapes—today's cottage style has attitude. Check out these sleek, molded-melamine chairs scooted up to a salvaged wood table, a sisal rug on wood floors, and the walls of clear glass doors designed to frame views. Rare are exuberant floral centerpieces. In their place are spare pots of succulents.

6 TWEAK TRADITION

right **Pair** a classic farm table with modern laminate chairs for a hip remix of traditional style. Create a cohesive design by repeating themes throughout. Here, black sharpens doors, chairs, and the chandelier. Balls on the chandelier recur in graphic circles in the rug and seat cushions.

A successful makeover isn't a clean sweep or a starting over. It's a reimagining of a space that combines the best of what you already own and adore with today's freshest looks.

Wallflowers they're not.
Walls today step forward as
canvases for expressing
your creativity through
paint, paper, even chalk.

ideas to steal

● Focus a pattern on
a single wall to keep
attention on the
design (it becomes
a piece of wall-size
art). It also avoids
overcrowding the
space visually.

● Ease into pattern
with stick-on decals.
More skilled? Try a
stencil or wallpaper.
For a stenciling
lesson, see page 184.

● Patterned walls
needn't be fussy.
Graphic styles of
traditional objects,
such as flowers in
tone-on-tone color
palettes, supply
modern verve.

<< ideas to steal

- Spiff up walls in chic painted stripes. Run stripes horizontally around a room to make the space feel wider; run them vertically to make a space seem taller.

- Avoid the look of a circus tent: Paint wide stripes in a soft, subdued combo of neutrals, such as this sand and cream.

- Painter's tape with edge blocker is a must for crisp painted lines. For a how-to lesson in painting stripes, see page 179.

<< ideas to steal

- Chalkboard paint is as easy to apply as ordinary latex paint and comes in dozens of colors.

- Apply it on one wall or all four, or above white wainscoting to produce sharp contrast.

- Use it in a sophisticated way as a giant menu board in a dining room or a playful way as an erasable canvas on a kid's room wall.

color | serving sizes

In small brushstrokes or large roll-ons, color transforms a room into a masterpiece. See how to use color in paint, fabric, and accessories.

Benjamin Moore
Outrageous Orange 2013-10

Benjamin Moore
Yellow Highlighter 2021-40

Fusion spray paint by Krylon
Spring Grass

refresh
Re-cover the seats of newly painted chairs with printed tea towels.

DRAMA QUEEN

left Focus color on one room feature for major impact and minimal money. Grass-green spray paint energizes these plain chairs. Choose fabrics and accessories that incorporate the green plus its color-wheel complements—orange-red and yellow—to boost intensity. A neutral background with putty walls, white trim, and woven shades keeps all eyes on the chairs.

refresh
For no-sew draperies, hem fabric with iron-on, fusible web, then hang by clip-on rings.

Sherwin-Williams
Frank Blue
SW 6967

Sherwin-Williams
Afternoon
SW 6675

Sherwin-Williams
Snowbound
SW 7004

REPEAT PLAYER
left Color repetition—such as the indigo in this room's textiles—moves the eye around a space for a pulled-together look. For lively tempo, vary the size of patterns; here, ikat appears large in drapes, small on seat cushions. Spotlight blue with sun-colored walls (it's a no-fail color combo). Give eyes a resting place with crisp white accent pieces.

refresh
Before painting wood furniture, wash it with a wood-safe cleaner and then protect it with two coats of primer.

What's the secret weapon of a hostess with the mostest? Tidy china cabinet storage that's pretty and put together no matter its size or shape.

SHELF SERVE
Stacked one atop the other, a pair of Parsons-style bookcases are just the right height to serve as a buffet table; their open, shadow box-like cubbies allow grab-and-go storage. Create a landscape of shape and color on the open shelves with neat stacks and groupings of serving pieces.

refresh
Baskets keep open shelving looking neat by corralling small items.

refresh
Modern color makes thrift-store finds suitable for today's rooms.

Not everything displayed in a hutch needs to be related to dining.

LET IT ROLL

above left **Attach casters to the feet of a side table, and you have a go-anywhere serving station. Use baskets to organize linens and glassware and maintain a tidy appearance on the open shelves.**

SECOND ACT

above right **A dated finish can ruin a perfectly good hutch. Give it a star turn with fresh paint and pattern. Gray-beige paint lends cool refinement to this piece, high-gloss white spray paint makes hardware pop, and a modern floral wallpaper lifts the hutch interior.**

TOUCH OF GLASS

right **Custom glass-front cabinets stretch almost to the ceiling, boosting storage space and vintage character. Chartreuse beaded-board backs visually connect the cabinets to the chairs. For a built-in look, slide ready-made bookcases or shelving units beside a window or doorway.**

Drummond
4055 Ovid Ave
Des Moines, IA
50310

entries

The front entry speaks volumes about your style. Make yours a shout-out of welcoming touches and smart storage solutions.

Time for Change. IN AN HOUR.

Personalize a foyer tabletop with art and found objects. We used a metal initial, a childhood toy, and a humble hinge for outgoing mail. Display pretty boxes, bowls, or trays on the table to use as stylish catchalls for sunglasses or smartphones. Under the table, conceal clumsy items such as footwear or sports gear in deep baskets. Stand umbrellas in a tall glazed garden pot. **IN AN AFTERNOON.** Hang a gallery of framed prints or family portraits. Relocate an upholstered side chair and a slim dresser or secretary to the foyer to make the space feel more like a cozy decorated room. A dresser that's 18 inches deep or less allows for foot traffic. Trick out a coat closet beside the back door with wall-to-wall hooks, baskets for hats and gloves, and a bench. Instead of a rug, lay colorful, durable carpet tiles that can be lifted up and washed in a sink or hosed down outside when muddied.

IN A WEEKEND. Add architecture to bare walls with chair rail molding installed 32 to 36 inches above the floor. Place a pair of candlestick lamps on a foyer table or hang plug-in sconces on either side of a mirror to add soft light, no electrician needed. Use wallpaper to change the look of a space. A bold print that could overwhelm a large room can brighten smaller areas—and brighten moods when friends and family enter the home.

before & after | first impressions

When the entry looks and feels more like a "keep out" sign than a welcome mat, it's time to update. The following fixes open possibilities.

before

STEP UP STYLE

above left **A scratched wood floor that never looks clean is a downer. Replace it with light-colored tile and a vibrant rug that is durable and brightens the space. These stair risers got a coat of white paint to complement the new banister, and the treads were stained to make them look as good as new.**

TAKE A SEAT

above right **A bench is a handy place to drop bags or sit when putting on shoes. What looks like pricey painted woodwork is actually a second layer of drywall, cut to create the effect of recessed panels. Wood molding finishes the edges.**

MAKE A SWITCH

opposite **A wood paneled door replaces the old metal one. Switching the direction makes better use of the space; now guests can easily step into the entry and close the door behind them. Slight irregularities on the surface of the limestone floor tiles disguise dirt.**

refresh
Swap dated floral wallpaper for neutral cream and gold paints to update a foyer's style.

try it | 4 great ideas

The front entry is a sneak peek into your home. Be gutsy with paint or wallpaper, and resourceful with space solutions.

refresh
Metallic wallpaper reflects light throughout a dark hallway.

1 BUREAU CHIEF

opposite **A chest of drawers adds a homey touch and stands in as storage for small gear. Update a vintage bureau with metallic paint, such as the electric blue here. Play up the paint's luster with galvanized-metal barn sconces.**

2 POWER TO THE PATTERN

above left **Green lattice wallpaper and white wainscoting take this entry from plain to wow. A diamond-pane door painted charcoal for contrast lets natural light stream in. Its dark hue is echoed in sconces and on a slender hall table.**

3 GREAT DIVIDE

above right **In a house without a foyer, a freestanding folding screen creates instant entry walls and a bit of privacy for an adjoining room. Tip: Equip upper panels of the screen with custom-cut mirrors.**

4 FABRIC SOFTENER

right **Lack a sizable entry or budget? Skirt the issue: Attach fabric to a bookcase using an adhesive-backed hook-and-loop tape to achieve an elegant entry table with ample room for hidden storage.**

style basics | on the wall

Know how to paint? Check. Able to drill holes? Check. Then put your entry walls to work with projects for hooks, memo boards, and more.

↖ ideas to steal

- Make wall hooks feel more like wall art. Add stature to a plain garment hook by first attaching it to a 1×4-inch wood block that has been painted with an edgy brushed-metal spray paint.

- Stagger the positions of hooks on a wall. It's not only practical—allowing longer hanging items to fit or for children to reach—but it also makes a graphic, sculptural statement.

- If modern isn't your style, take a piece of salvaged wood—old barn board, crown molding, or door pediment—and fasten a row of coat hooks to its front.

The space just inside the door is only for the things you use daily that merit prominent storage spots. Sports equipment needs to air out: stow that gear in the garage or on the porch.

>> ideas to steal

- Deal with the stuff that gets dumped upon arrival: Create an efficient drop zone beside even the tightest entry door. First, hang a sectioned bin to provide specific spots for family members and pets. Include mini drawers to collect coupons, gift cards, and school forms.

- Install oversize wall clips to hold important papers that require immediate action. Stash footwear on the floor in a crate or bin.

- Transform the wall into a spot for daily reminders with dry-erase paint. Mount a magnetic, dry-erase board to the back of the door to track schedules and reminders.

<< ideas to steal

- Create a message board that dovetails with your decor. If you're a fan of cottage style, transform a vintage frame, salvaged window, or collection of serving trays into a message center. Fill its open area with corkboard or dry-erase paint.

- Make messaging more attractive. Magnetic spray paint topped by erasable chalkboard paint in a bright color gets your message seen and heard loud and clear.

- Maintain a tidy look on your board by swapping ordinary magnets for bedazzling ones made by gluing small magnets to the backs of vintage earrings or buttons.

idea gallery | back entries

It's sloppy. It's full of traffic. It's the hardest-working area of your home. Make every inch of your back entry count with smart function and good looks.

UNDER SERVED

opposite **Even a sliver of space at the back door can live large. In this entry into a kitchen, a nook serves as a minimalist mudroom thanks to a row of coat hooks and a built-in bench with storage inside.**

DIVIDE TO CONQUER

right **To manage a family's storage needs, build a coat closet with tall, locker-like compartments on top and cubbies on bottom. Build cubbies tall and deep enough to double as a bench. Line the back wall with fun wallpaper.**

refresh

Full-extension drawer glides make shoes easy to reach, even those tucked way back.

If utter chaos greets you at the back door, stop the insanity. Just a few hooks and baskets get kids (and spouses) trained to put gear away upon arrival.

storage | furniture fix-ups

Park a furniture piece near a busy entry and convert it into headquarters for the stuff of daily life.

refresh
A mirror equipped with hooks makes keys easy to find.

TAKE YOUR PLACE
Divide a console table into zones. Start below by sorting footwear or outgoing items in deep baskets. Make papers easy to grab with a standing file holder on the tabletop. Dock electronics on a charging station. A hook added to the desk holds a purse.

Simplify your coming and going with an organization station.

INSIDE STORY

above left **Remove a shelf to tuck in a shredder and destroy unwanted mail as you open it. Gather bills to pay in a prominent spot such as a hanging pocket. Put labeled spare keys on magnetic hooks.**

CLEAR CHOICE

above right **Stack shoeboxes as holding tanks for school papers. Turn a door into a bulletin board with magnetic strips.**

HIDDEN HQ

right **Sort mail into the wine rack of a buffet. Label one cubby per family member. Keep often-referenced papers in binders, one per person or purpose. Mount the family calendar in a frame with glass removed.**

kitchens

Reviving the look of the busiest room in the house needn't be time-consuming and expensive. Try these affordable and stylish tricks.

Time for Change. IN AN HOUR.

Line shelves and drawers with patterned papers. (Tip: Use durable liners in drawers and more elegant papers under dishware.) Hang pretty kitchen towels on clip rings and slide them onto a rod to dress up the window above the sink. Center a floor runner in front of the kitchen sink to add colorful pattern. **IN AN AFTERNOON.** Sort kitchen gear using the same decision-making process as a closet purge: Donate equipment you seldom use and discard food items past their use-by date. Replace hardware on kitchen cabinets using knobs or pulls that fit existing screw holes. Install a new light fixture with a dimmer switch so you can change lighting levels as desired. Create a memo center by brushing blackboard paint on a cabinet door interior; add peel-and-stick cork inside the opposite door. **IN A WEEKEND.** Remove a few upper cabinets to reduce the utilitarian feel; replace them with open shelves on brackets. Or take off only the doors and replace them with glass-front doors. Swap a kitchen table and chairs for an island and stools to add counter space without losing a lunch spot. Paint island cabinetry a bold fun hue, such as berry blue or cool mango. (Tip: Use a liquid deglosser to remove residue of cleaners and oils before applying primer.) Freshen the backsplash by installing glass tiles in a classic subway style.

before & after | save to splurge

Curling laminate? Worn cabinets? What to do? Smart strategies and affordable products saved this kitchen in style.

refresh
Buy new wood letters at a crafts store and paint them a fun shade.

before

ISLAND LIVING

above left **Rather than waiting to remodel, the couple decided to refresh. They started by building a bigger island, topping a vintage base with a granite top. The granite cost just a few hundred dollars more than laminate thanks to smart shopping.**

SMART BUYS

above right **Durable laminate flooring offers a budget-friendly option to solid wood floors. The owners nabbed a great deal on their secondhand (but hardly used) appliances by checking Craigslist several times a day.**

BLACK BEAUTY

opposite **Existing cabinets painted black, a subway tile backsplash, and granite countertops rejuvenate the once dated kitchen. These savvy homeowners lived with the kitchen for a few years and worked out penny-wise solutions before spending money.**

refresh
Rectangular stools are easier to tuck under a narrow ledge than round ones.

before & after | out of the woods

Oak cabinets, oak floors, and giant oak trees looming out the windows kept this kitchen in the dark. Learn how it lightened up.

SPACE GAIN

above **Pushing one wall back 24 inches made way for a row of cabinets. Above the molding, standard materials—4×8-foot siding panels and pine boards— customize the ceiling. Boards nailed to the soffit give the cabinetry a custom look.**

BRUSHWORK

opposite **Paint—classic white and whale gray—transformed the cabinets. For a smooth paint finish, use a high-quality primer, a self-leveling topcoat, and a mohair roller. Marble-look countertops and butcher block replace dated ceramic tile.**

before

refresh

**Add eye hooks
to wood balls
and hang them
like fringe from
Roman shades.**

The kitchen works such long hours that it runs the risk of looking tired. These design pick-me-ups can give it fresh appeal.

refresh
Cone-shape shades with brown velvet trim give pendants a look similar to table lamps.

refresh

Tuck kitchen shelves in an alcove to hide them from view.

1 WATER IT DOWN

opposite **A palette of soft watery colors gives this new kitchen a dressy look. That's a smart strategy when a kitchen is open to the living spaces. The dark mahogany furniture-look island and green tile backsplash support the theme.**

2 MAKE IT MODERN

above left **Energetic blue paint and modern pulls are easy age erasers for dated cabinets. Crisp white laminate countertops, walls, and shelves stabilize the intense blue, a trick to keep in mind if you plan to use bright color.**

3 GIVE IT TEXTURE

above right **Here's proof that neutrals with texture deliver touchable style. Wood planks clad the ceiling and walls; sleek laminate paves the counters. Accessories, such as rattan stools and an iron pot rack, are opposites that attract.**

4 REPEAT IT

right **A modern kitchen in a vintage home—and an old table paired with modern chairs—illustrates the importance of repeating elements to create a cohesive look. The same is true of color: Blues and greens go on and on.**

style basics | dining nooks

Simple changes in your space can create a special place for meals that complements your kitchen's style.

<< ideas to steal

● Stretched for dining space? A bench takes much less room than chairs. Up the functionality with storage underneath. Look for ready-made benches or build one yourself using cabinetry designed for above a refrigerator.

● Use a small table with leaves and slim chairs to maximize space for the possibility of adding guests on occasion.

● Opt for a soft color palette that mixes with white to calm the mood.

>> ideas to steal

● Paint a wall using tinted blackboard paint and let your kids do the decorating. Unleash their inner artists with a stack of colored chalk and an eraser.

● Install a series of shelves on the wall. Use narrower white shelves to hold eating supplies and art gear.

● Add a deeper shelf to use as a breakfast bar. (This one measures about 11×75 inches.) Tuck stools under the counter.

color | bold strokes

Injecting color into a kitchen requires clear thinking. Use color where it's easy and affordable to redo if you change your mind.

Valspar
Dylan Velvet
3008-5B

Benjamin Moore
Slate Teal
2058-20

SUNSHINE CENTRAL

above **A happy shade of yellow turns the island into a hardworking focal point. Teal stools complement the yellow, and a fabric-covered lampshade repeats the two hues. White cabinets provide a neutral backdrop for punches of color.**

TROPICAL PUNCH

opposite **Warm coral and cool aqua are complementary colors that play well together. In this breakfast area, the colors are used in the same value so they create balance. Neutral woodwork and floors become visual resting spots.**

Martha Stewart Living
Sunken Pool
MSL126

Sherwin-Williams
Emotional
SW 6621

refresh
Painted narrow
wall spaces
create the look of
horizontal stripes
above and below a
bank of windows.

Open up a kitchen by replacing some upper cabinets with handy shelves.

refresh
Lean framed prints against the wall for a gallery look.

GRAPHIC STRIPES
Two blocky white shelves serve as a counterpoint to vivid floral wallpaper. The contrast between materials adds a modern note. Varying the shape and size of the shelves adds interest to the wall.

Make sure shelves are engineered to hold the weight of heavy items.

VERTICAL STORAGE

above left **A country-style plate rack above the sink becomes a shelf with vertical storage. It speeds cleanup too. Wet dishes slot into the rack to dry in place until dinnertime; any drips end up in the sink below.**

PERFECT GEOMETRY

above right **Shelves in pairs double storage and vintage charm. These stainless-steel shelves and black iron brackets replaced original upper cabinets. This strategy works to open up space in a small kitchen with adequate storage.**

MODERN SLABS

right **Floating, open-air wood shelves aren't what they seem. Look closer: Thin wire cables thread through the outside corners of the shelves for support. Installed on sleek tile, the look is modern and rustic.**

bedrooms

Packed schedules and long to-do lists can result in sleepless nights, so create a soothing dream haven and bring on your slumber.

Time for Change. IN AN HOUR.

Remake the bed with fresh linens: lightweight cottons for summer, and flannel and wool for winter. Add a handsome bolster pillow to contrast with bed pillows. Move the bed to face the best view—of a window, furniture piece, or wall arrangement. Organize the nightstand by placing a tray on top to hold bedside items. For comfortable seating, place an upholstered bench at the foot of the bed. Use a painted wood chair as an unexpected bedside table. **IN AN AFTERNOON.** Paint the headboard a warm, rich color, such as slate-teal. In a small bedroom hang a shelf in place of a bedside table and a sconce instead of a table lamp. Replace the window treatment with a room-darkening Roman shade and curtain panels that measure 2 to 2½ times the window's width for a billowing romantic look. Rearrange the bed on top of a new rug. (Tip: The rug should extend beyond the bed at least 24 inches on both sides and at the foot.) **IN A WEEKEND.** Add pattern to the headboard wall by painting a base coat and stenciling a second color on top. Use colors with minimal contrast to add serenity. (Tip: Search the Internet for "wall stencils." These bold oversize patterns are easy to use.) Create a canopy by installing curtain rods from the ceiling in a rectangle slightly larger than the bed; hang curtain panels at each corner.

before & after | *suite spot*

A low ceiling, awkward slopes, and only one place for the bed challenged one homeowner to reimagine the bedroom.

WINDOW VIEW
above left Furniture arrangement was one of the room's biggest challenges. The solution? Place the bed in front of the windows—with an open-lattice headboard to let in the light. Cozy up the space with a canopy attached to the ceiling; curtains hang from all four corners.

FUNCTIONAL FLAIR
above right The wall-ceiling slopes provided an easy division of space. This alcove serves as a cozy reading area. Cubbies fitted with baskets hide books. For added privacy, a damask curtain panel matching the bed canopy can be pulled to hide the area.

PATTERN PLAY
opposite A mix of patterns in the same color palette unites while defining functions. A subtle stripe on the wood floors unifies the odd-shape room. The wallpaper in the alcove separates that space from the main bedroom, and the bed's blue-and-cream curtains signify the sleeping zone.

refresh
Painting walls
and ceiling in
one neutral tone
minimizes odd
angles and the
feel of a low
ceiling.

before & after | classic retreat

Simplified sitting and sleeping areas and a neutral color scheme give this large bedroom a sense of calm.

FUNCTION FIRST

above left **The first step to finding balance? Figure out how to divide the bedroom into functional areas. The new bedroom's simplicity focuses on a sleeping area and relaxed seating in front of the fireplace. A desk was relocated to another room.**

ALL IN THE DETAILS

above right **Attention to detail defines the space. The muted mix of patterns on the chairs pillows, and drapes add charm without being overwhelming.**

SERENITY NOW

opposite **A serene color scheme gives the bedroom a new look. The tufted bench with nailhead trim, and fluted and carved details on the bed frame lend elegance and luxury to this personal haven. Neutral walls and flooring offer a simple backdrop.**

refresh
Add sophistication to the bedroom with metallic hardware and classic pleated draperies.

Personal touches and convenience go a long way when remaking a bedroom into a relaxing sanctuary.

1 ROMANTIC LINES

opposite An under-eave bedroom with board-and-batten walls and a tongue-and-groove ceiling is a lesson in lines. The striped rug and bedding echo the pattern. Bursts of red mix with gray for a relaxed ambience with a little energy.

2 WAKE-UP CALL

above left Keepsake furniture sets a nostalgic mood in a bedroom. Use paint to wake up the sleepy style of a vintage bed and nightstand (prime them before painting). Spread color with fun fabrics for curtains, pillows, and bedding.

3 STYLISH STORAGE

above right Pretty bedding and soft surfaces deliver live-in comfort, but here it's the storage that shines. Inch for inch, built-in cabinetry adds more storage and more seating in less space. Doors on the cabinets can hide bedding or a television set.

4 WINTER WHITES

right This farmhouse bedroom features classic board-and-batten siding done up in white. The trick is to choose warm whites with a touch of yellow. Add character with oversize, dramatic shapes, such as a four-poster bed.

5

A mix of styles and finishes, such as modern, classic, or hand-me-down, makes a room look collected and personal—not predictable.

5 STYLE QUEST
above **A traditional bed stars in this bedroom makeover. Modern flourishes in the graphic wallpaper, lacquered nightstands, and Hollywood Regency stools contrast with the bed and at the same time make it look perfectly stylish.**

6 WONDERFUL WOODS
opposite **Consider these unconventional pairings that deliver personal style: a traditional desk used as a nightstand and a twiggy sconce, sleek aqua pottery and embroidered aqua pillows, and a streamlined bench next to a traditional four-poster.**

style basics | nightstands

Write your own rules regarding what makes a good nightstand. Experiment with size, shape, and accessories before you commit.

refresh

Look up! That bluish-green ceiling adds a surprising touch to a bedroom.

>> ideas to steal

- Style should be the first requirement for a nightstand. This antique Moorish inlaid-wood table adds an exotic touch.

- Second, maximize space. There's room on this small hexagon for a swirly lamp, glasses, a cell phone, and a book.

- Other antique pieces with tabletop space, such as a desk or dresser, also make good nightstands.

<< ideas to steal

- A circular nightstand provides plenty of opportunity for creative display. And you're sure to find a size that will fit your bedroom.

- Skirt the table with a slipcover; a glass circle protects the table's surface. The green band with gold fringe repeats the drapery treatment.

- A sleek and skinny lamp base adds style without taking up too much space.

>> ideas to steal

- Before you buy a nightstand, list what style and size you want and what items you want to keep on it. Make sure it partners well with the bed's headboard style.

- A small wicker table adds a vintage look and continues the blue color scheme of the wallpaper and headboard.

- Select accessories that tell a story. This modern lamp and bedding add a youthful feel.

storage | beyond closets

Bedroom closets need to hold a lot of stuff. Learn how to rethink storage options to suit your space needs.

OFF THE WALL

Organize one wall of a generous walk-in closet using kitchen cabinets. Upper cabinets, only 12 inches deep, sit on 24-inch-deep base cabinets. Canvas boxes and drawer dividers maintain order. A mirror anchors the dressing nook.

Maintain everything from shoes to rings in a handy storage center.

FILE SMART
above left Keep your shoes under cover and within reach using this shallow shoe storage center that features flip-down bins. Label drawers to identify the contents.

ADDED VALUE
above right Hang basic shoe-care instructions in your closet. Download and print out advice for leather, suede, canvas, and fabric shoes at *BHG.com/ shoecare*. Assemble and box care kits to keep your footware in top shape.

CARE CENTRAL
right Shoes are a big investment. Keep them in tip-top shape by dedicating a bedroom or closet corner to their care. To create some personal space, combine a dressing table with shelves and bins.

before & after | european roots

Weathered wood, shades of pewter gray and cream, and woven textures transform a cramped, outdated powder room into a Belgian beauty.

ART GALLERY

above left **Narrow and dark, this 3×8-foot powder room felt like a cramped closet. To give the illusion of more space, walls were brightened with a warm cream paint. Black-and-white photographs, unified by black frames and white matting, hang on all walls, creating an upscale, gallery-like effect.**

LIGHT RIGHT

above right **When choosing lighting for a room, tie its shape and finish to other elements in the space. This ceiling fixture's brushed-chrome finish and curvy supports complement the vanity's aged gray paint finish and open sides. Its dark hue melds with the black-and-white photography.**

SPACE SAVER

opposite **A stock vanity would have been too large for the powder room, and a custom one too costly. Instead, a slim wood table purchased for $150 was outfitted with a petite vessel sink. Its aged patina and X-motif styling resemble a pricey Belgian antique. Limited countertop space made a wall-mounted faucet necessary. Open shelving makes baskets and bowls easy to access.**

before

refresh

Refinish a thrift shop mirror with a few coats of aged pewter and antique gold paints.

before & after | *classic charmer*

By replacing the vanity and adding traditional details, a 1990s powder room shows off in pretty 1920s style.

before

BRIGHT IDEA

above left **For a fresh take on lighting, classic candlestick lamps were wired through the vanity's marble top. The lamps' softer glow is acceptable since the space isn't used for daily primping and prepping. A wood mirror in traditional style, relocated from another room, now bounces light around the small space.**

TAP THE PAST

above right **Layers of detail infuse the room with the look of an earlier era. The single-handle faucet was reused from the old powder room because its water-pump shape and enameled tap recapture the past yet still feel current.**

SHOW SOME LEG

opposite **The previous vanity, a repurposed dresser, crowded the powder room, but its furniture style had appeal. A new table-like vanity built from off-the-shelf millwork pieces, including turned legs, provides an airier look and feel. The base is stained dark walnut to contrast with the white tile. Carrara marble tops off the classic look.**

refresh

Wallpaper is a great way to add color and pattern to a room. Go bold in rooms where you don't spend a lot of time.

try it| 4 great ideas

Basic elements can leave a bathroom
feeling a little cold. Warm it up with color,
pattern, and character.

1 FLIRT WITH COLOR

opposite **Accessories give this basic bathroom a fun personality. Look for a shower curtain to set the color scheme—here, bright yellow and gray. Bring in yellow's complementary hue of blue for an energetic splash. A tray table organizes shower supplies.**

2 POWER UP WHITE

above left **Here's proof that basic white need not be boring. Raised panels on the cabinet, an open space on the bottom filled with baskets, and a handsome black countertop give this vanity plenty of style. A twig mirror adds unexpected contrast.**

3 GO GEOMETRIC

above right **Geometric shapes give a bath a sophisticated edge. Repeat the shapes, such as the curved mirror and étagère, to prevent a space from feeling too busy. The wallpaper's soft tones create a more subtle background than a high-contrast pattern would.**

4 GET NATURAL

right **A stained wood vanity and an oversize mirror anchor this room with rustic appeal. Without doors on the vanity front, personal items under the counter stay within easy reach. Wire baskets contain towels near the shower and repeat the metal tones of sconces and faucets.**

style basics | terrific tile

Tile works its magic in any bathroom by introducing texture, color, and pattern. The options are limitless.

⌃ ideas to steal

- Start by playing with tile. A mixture of shapes, sizes, tones, and textures adds interest.

- Determine how you want to use patterned tiles. They create a horizontal band here and can add pattern to the floor.

- Select the shape and installation method for the field tile. These round tiles come premounted on square sheets that make installation a breeze.

⌃ ideas to steal

- White, black, and gray tiles make vintage style look new again.

- First decide where to use the black tiles. Here they create horizontal stripes on the wall and a medallion pattern on the floor.

- Use different shapes on walls and floors to define each. This bath uses subway tiles with accents on walls and all hexagonal tiles in different colors on the floor.

ideas to steal

- Think outside the shower walls. Multicolor tiles slip beyond the tub to create an unbroken canvas that visually expands a small bathroom.

- Choose tiles in a range of favorite colors. These blues and greens go from light to bold to create a one-of-a-kind look.

- Support a bold tiled wall with accessories in coordinating solid colors.

Bath storage has to make room for it all—
from bulky towels to delicate glass bottles.

STACK IT
Unfinished wood crates treated to a color wash stack up as colorful and adaptable bathroom storage. Screws hold the crates together and to the wall. Make sure the crates are strong enough to hold what you want to store.

refresh
Slip a bench into the bathroom for seating or stacking.

Let easy accessibility be the guiding principle for bath storage.

STRETCH UP

above left **In small rooms, usable square footage often stretches up. Take advantage of this by incorporating ready-to-assemble tall units with open rows of hooks. The net effect? Handsome storage for towels, toiletries, and supplies.**

MAKE IT GRAPHIC

above right **The simple structure of this tall bookcase instantly organizes clutter. Each niche holds similar items; slip a basket into one niche to contain lots of small items. Make sure to attach the bookcase to the wall.**

SHOW IT OFF

right **A folding tray table serves as a handy landing surface in the bathroom. A clear glass canister offers pretty storage for soap. An assortment of glass canisters for small items, including cotton balls and nail polish, works too.**

work spaces

Organized. Versatile. Stylish. Let those three descriptive words define the areas where you catch up on bills, wrap gifts, or supervise homework.

Time for Change. IN AN HOUR.

Toss clutter; sort usable items into cutlery baskets or trays that fit inside drawers. Keep pencils, pens, and markers handy by stashing them in a trio of pretty containers. Purchase a decorative basket or bin for recycling. Sort papers into colorful file folders; stash them in wall-hung magazine holders. Set up a charging station in a desktop tray; add a multiplug for handheld devices. **IN AN AFTERNOON.** Hang a collection of favorite photos in an organized grid on one wall. Create an inspiration board by covering corkboard with pretty fabric; pin a collection of treasured cards, photos, and magazine pages on the board.

Empty the storage closet; refill with purchased storage boxes sized to fit. Fill the boxes and add labels so it's easy to find what you need. Pop off the chair seat, and wrap and staple new fabric around it. **IN A WEEKEND.** Paint one wall with colorful chalkboard paint; invite family and friends to sketch on the new wall. Or try whiteboard paint for a finish that makes it easy to clean up after using dry-erase markers. Rehab a worn desk with fresh color and top the desk with glass for a durable, easy-clean surface. Give metal file cabinets a new look by spray-painting them with a colorful and glossy finish. Replace a ceiling light fixture with a chandelier above a desk or table.

before & after | *work suite*

The "everything for everyone" home office makes space for kids, crafts, and paperwork. Lots of table area keeps everyone happy.

before

READING NOOK
above left **For a perfect spot for reading, it's hard to beat this freestanding bench topped with a custom cushion. Bins below provide easy access to storage so kids can put things away. The palette of yellow, aqua, bright green, cobalt, and chocolate repeats the colors used in the rest of the house.**

STORAGE REHAB
above right **A repurposed painted console serves as storage for supplies. Tension rods hold the curtain panels in place. Outdoor mailboxes hung on the wall, bins, and buckets make clever supply caddies. Carpet tiles offer a soft, colorful base; damaged tiles are easy to replace.**

FOR ONE AND ALL
opposite **White walls serve as a foil for bold color in this home office. One wall is equipped with a swath of yellow laminate countertops, movable file cabinets, and shelf storage. The centered table adjusts to low for kid art projects, and high and tilted for grownup art projects.**

refresh

Prefer to remain uncommitted? Choose pure white for shelves and add jolts of color with fun accents.

try it | 6 great ideas

Nothing says your work space can't be fun as well as functional. These ideas go to work for you, your family, and your home.

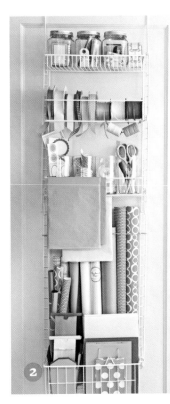

1 SETTLE DOWN

opposite **A tabletop perched on two filing cabinets turns a corner of a room into a sewing center. Buy new file cabinets or repurpose ones you already own. Purchase a wood plank at a home center; attach it to the cabinets using L brackets.**

2 WRAP STATION

above left **Think a dedicated gift-wrap space is a large-house luxury? Think again. This sturdy over-the-door rack is designed to hold cans and boxes in a pantry, but it's perfect for corralling ribbons and papers too.**

3 STOW AWAY

above right **The secret to a home office is building storage in each and every nook. Above-refrigerator cabinets provide the base for this window seat; doors offer easy access to the compartments.**

4 FAMILY PLAN

right **Everyone in the family has a place to work in this multiuse office. Flanking closets provide space for computer work on one side and sewing on the other. A large centered table offers plenty of surface area for rolling out a big crafts project.**

refresh
Modernize a worn oak table with an eye-popping shade of paint.

refresh
Multiples—three-ring binders, woven baskets, locker bins—always look orderly when stored together.

5 CORNER OFFICE

opposite An L-shape desk provides maximum efficiency. It puts file cabinets and work space within easy reach and offers plenty of room for files on the counter. Accessories, such as a colorful rug and artwork, impart a warm, homey feeling.

6 DESIGN CENTRAL

right An office tucked into the corner of a living room has to maintain a stylish outlook and keep clutter under control while providing access to supplies. A wall of storage cubbies organizes gear. The desk can turn into a dining spot when needed.

Vary materials to make an office feel like home. Sleek laminate, woven baskets, and burnished metal showcase one winning combination.

storage | wall works

Have room for only a desk? Never fear. Put the empty wall above and around it to work for stashing items easily and artfully.

FRAME IT
Organize crafting, scrapbooking, or decorating projects by outfitting a series of oversize frames with corkboard backing. Hang the frames on a wall above the desk; pin ideas to the boards for daily inspiration.

Mix pretty and practical to create an office that's fun to use.

HANG IT

above left **Metal pegboard might seem more at home above a workbench, but this functional product makes sense even above the prettiest desk. Movable accessories, such as shelves and brackets, let you customize to suit your needs.**

SHELVE IT

above right **Desks and shelves make stylish yet hardworking companions. Add a single shelf for easy access or a wall of shelves to maximize vertical space. Make sure each shelf can support its load.**

STACK IT

right **Create a work center by stacking a shelf unit on top of a desk; secure on the back using L brackets. File loose papers inside pretty file folders tucked into wall-mounted magazine holders.**

outdoor spaces

Turn a patio or porch into an extension of your house with weather-resistant products that bring indoor style outdoors.

Time for Change. IN AN

HOUR. Pop potted plants into pretty containers and spread them around an outdoor seating area. Place a colorful rug on the porch or deck floor; choose a UV-coated polypropylene rug for durability outside. Toss oversize pillows on the floor for lounging—use weather-resistant pillow forms and fabrics. Cluster a collection of votives on a tray or spread them along a deck railing. **IN AN AFTERNOON.** Give dull plastic garden furniture new life by spraying it with paint formulated for use on plastic. Add interior appeal and a little privacy to a porch by hanging indoor-outdoor curtain panels around the perimeter of the space; use plastic rope as curtain tiebacks. Hang lanterns from porch posts or between windows on a three-season porch. Set up for entertaining by adding a narrow shelf to one side of the porch; keep trays and baskets on top for table gear. **IN A WEEKEND.** Give a plain porch floor the decorator treatment by painting it in a checkerboard pattern or adding a large-scale stencil pattern. (Use porch and deck enamel on the floor to ensure the painted finish will look good for several years.) Paint the ceiling sky blue to simulate the effect of looking up at a summer sky. Update seat cushions with slipcovers that are weather-resistant and washable. Create a soothing breeze on a porch by installing a ceiling fan.

A minty-green sunroom once clashed with nature. Now, it's color-happy with a palette of summery tones and a design-smart, relaxing furniture plan.

before

TRUNK SHOW

above Three trunks scooted together form an L-shape window seat; cushions keep them comfy. Painting the window trim the same color as the walls moves the eyes outside rather than stopping them at the window trim. Roller shades painted with stripes resemble awnings.

HAPPILY EVER AFTER

left Aqua, grass green, coral, and sandy yellow set a summery mood. Furniture pulled into a U-shape sitting area invites conversation. A rug sets off the main gathering spot, and an oversize ottoman works as a footrest and coffee table.

YOUR SERVE
A console table opposite the window seat transforms into a bar or buffet when needed. New ceiling medallions aged with brown shoe polish add architectural interest on the wall. Accessories introduce shape and pattern to the vignette.

refresh
Woven mats nailed to the wall with brads provide a textural backdrop.

before & after | *deck duty*

This deck capitalizes on its possibilities with defined, inviting places for gardening, grilling, and chilling.

before

CHILL ZONE

above left **Move your living room to the deck for summertime relaxing. Cushioned furniture encourages lingering. Containers of ornamental grasses and pots on the deck rail stand tall to create room-like walls. A weatherproof rug looks like sisal but is softer on bare feet.**

POTTING CENTRAL

above right **A sturdy workbench is the perfect multitasker. Place it in a handy location by the back door and make sure it includes storage space for tools, a shelf to hold pots and soil, and a work surface.**

SMART STORAGE

inset **Tuck bamboo trays inside drawers to organize small tools and gloves. Extra drawers can hold entertaining supplies, such as candles, napkins, and napkin rings.**

CHEF'S CORNER

opposite **Create an outdoor cooking station next to the grill to prevent nonstop traipsing to the kitchen. Adjustable metal pantry shelves provide storage and a work surface. Metal locker bins hold barbecue tools and dish towels—and serve as handy totes for dirty dishes when dinner is done.**

refresh
Keep fresh herbs within reach in improvised planters, such as this galvanized wine rack.

before & after | *porch reform*

Insider design secrets helped this front porch shift from easy-to-overlook to must-see. The L-shape porch works with fresh-air style.

SWING AWAY
above left **The narrow end of the L-shape porch provides a perfect spot for swinging. Curtain panels, stenciled with swallows in flight, provide a bit of privacy from a nearby street. Use exterior acrylic paint for the stencils to ensure their durability.**

SET THE TABLE
above right **This narrow metal desk features weather-resistant paint. Roll it in front of the bench for dining for two; pull up chairs and stools to make room for a crowd. Pushed up to the wall, it also serves as a drink station.**

PARTY PORCH
opposite **Once wide open to view, this porch benefits from curtains with oversize grommets that create movable walls for sun control and privacy. The lightweight double-duty furnishings move as needed. The green table on casters (*above*) rolls from around the corner to serve as a dining spot; the tree stumps on casters (*above*) double as handy side tables or stools.**

before

refresh
Rugs add an indoor vibe to an outdoor location.

When warm weather arrives, living space expands. Try these ideas for turning an open-air space into party central.

refresh

Oversize bouquets—tall or wide—make a statement in an outdoor space.

1 SWEET SPOT

opposite A playful attitude injects fun pattern and color into a porch party. Paper parasols create an inexpensive faux chandelier. Pretty flowers, real ones in bowls and illustrated ones scattered on the tablecloth, bring summer style to the table.

2 RUSTIC REFINED

above right A weathered copper-top table with scrolled iron on the base introduces a dressy note to this deck. The metal candelabra pair up to create a dramatic gesture. Woven plastic chairs look like wicker but stand up to sun and water.

3 TOP IT OFF

right A pergola provides just enough structure to turn a deck into a backyard retreat. Curtain panels soften the edges and introduce privacy while soft seating makes one want to linger. Box cushions teamed with a low table create dining space.

color | from the garden

Inspiration for outdoor color grows all around, from the veggie patch to the flower border. Use sky, water, rock, and soil hues to ground the palette.

FLORAL BOUQUET
left **Select the colors for a porch based on a favorite flower border. Use a cherished hue in the largest amounts; add drops of other colors as accents. Here, pink and salmon set the mood with pops of lemon yellow and fuchsia.**

Sherwin-Williams
Tuberose
SW 6578

Sherwin-Williams
Daffodil
SW 6901

refresh
Unify a collection of mismatched furniture with a coat of white paint.

Martha Stewart Living
Whetstone Gray MSL258

Benjamin Moore
Jupiter Glow 021

ORANGE DROPS

left Think of neutral backgrounds—the putty floor and gray shutters—as the soil, and rock that anchor landscapes. The bursts of orange demand attention, much like poppies waving in the breeze. This porch faces the sunset, so the warm hues reflect the evening sky.

refresh
Use a putty shade to mimic the look of a gravel path in the garden.

house tours

Think of a whole-house project as marathon decorating. Each completed room propels you toward a goal of establishing your decorating style and enhancing life at home.

classic colorful cottage

DESK RESET
In the bedroom's corner office, a thick display ledge hangs above a shapely 1800s desk revived with cobalt spray paint. New large floral fabric on the chair seat balances with draperies stitched from 1960s fabric.

refresh
Leftover paints applied with an eyedropper to a stretched canvas yield a Jackson Pollock effect.

before

cottage color

With soothing hues, strong pattern, and cherished antiques,
a home is transformed into a personal work of art.

What She Did. This 1930s

cottage had good bones: classic molding, wood floors, rounded archways, and oak cabinetry. Only cosmetic changes were needed. So, treating her home like a blank canvas, the owner filled it with the colors, fabrics, and objects she loves. The result is a pretty place to call home and a calming retreat.

TO KICK OFF THE MAKEOVER, the homeowner established neutral backgrounds, painting walls gray, staining floors dark walnut, and slipcovering furniture in white canvas. Next, she layered on her favorites: milk glass, antique furnishings with curvaceous shapes, the color blue. She repeated these elements throughout the 930-square-foot space to yield a cohesive look. Ceilings were painted sky blue, taupe, and gray to add dimension.

NEW FIXTURES REFERENCE THE PAST, from a pedestal sink in the bath to the subway tile backsplash in the kitchen. Existing kitchen cabinets were painted, and shelf brackets were added beneath upper cabinets. Wood pedestal feet attached to the toe-kick evoke the tailored look of furniture.

MIXING IN THE MODERN prevents the look from becoming stale or sweet. Bold patterns appear in fabrics, including the bed's headboard slipcover and pillows, wallpaper, and do-it-yourself artwork. Doses of black add edgy sophistication.

SWEET SPOT
White paint rehabilitates and integrates mismatched side chairs in the dining room. The pure geometric shapes of the X-leg desk and pedestal table offer modern balance. A crystal chandelier adds glam, and a flirty floral wallpaper sweetens the space.

before:

SIMPLE STYLE

above left **Keeping foundation pieces neutral—a white sofa and wood floor, for instance—allows the living room to be updated on a whim with fresh pillows and throw rugs. The side tables are fashioned from wire wastebaskets and round wood tabletops from a home center.**

BLUE HEAVEN

above right **A playful balance of patterns— oversize gingham draperies, Suzani pillows, a bold floral area rug—keeps the eye moving around the living room. They are united by the color blue; the mismatched armchairs have the common element of beige slipcovers.**

Country strong

Fade to black: Contrasting black window sashes bring strength and sophistication to a country look. Brush black paint on picture frames, interior doors, and bookcases as well.

Round it out: A pedestal table adds refined shape beside a bed and in seating areas, such as the living room.

Splurge on elegance: An updated fireplace grounds a room in style, making it the jewel of the room. New marble tiles are an easy way to cover up an outdated or distracting surround.

refresh
Enliven one wall with wallpaper that ties to the colorful accents in the room.

CLEAR SEA
The kitchen's oak base cabinets were painted black and the uppers white for contrast. Custom glass-panel doors ordered online replace solid doors; stained glass the color of beach glass fills in their panes.

UNDER COVER

above **A slipcover for the headboard easily changes a bed's look.** Blues, sour yellow, white, and black repeat in the bedroom to tie the scene together. A wicker chair and floors painted with white porch enamel relax this room with country styling.

LIGHT IDEAS

top right **To visually stretch space in a tiny bath, choose light-reflecting surfaces such as a French door outfitted with frosted window film, or white tile floors, or beaded-board paneling.**
middle right **For an even lighter feel, a pedestal sink takes up less floor space than a vanity.**

before

refresh Simply framed vintage prints repeat the theme of vintage made modern.

BEDDING BOUNTY

above left Foundation pieces on the bed—sheets, duvet, and bed skirt—provide a neutral palette for pillows, throws, and accessories. Replace a few pieces, and the bedroom has an entirely new attitude.

METAL AND WOOD

top left The master bath pairs mirrored metal medicine cabinets with weathered-oak washstands. Covered baskets on the washstands hide clutter. Walls pick up gray from the home's palette.

COZY CORNER

above A sloping ceiling and a comfy chair and ottoman make perfect companions in the master bedroom. The chair maintains the neutral background while a dramatic pillow adds pops of color in yellow and gray.

MEDIA DIGS
Original stone walls give the renovated basement a striking background; new laminate floors warm up the space. Cozy seating makes this a handy hangout for watching television or listening to music.

refresh
Play with scale by introducing an oversize lampshade for dramatic effect.

contemporary raised ranch

COMPACT COMFORT A deep sectional solves the space problem in a cozy living room. Minimize the visual impact of seating by choosing pieces in a color slightly lighter than the wall color. Accessories add color and pattern.

before

modern by design

This revamped house went from oh-so-boring to warm and modern, with space that's smart, spare, and family-friendly.

What They Did. The house on the market lacked personality but had a great floor plan for a family (living spaces up and bedrooms down). Plus, its good location vaulted it to first choice for these young, first-time homeowners. Fast-forward past the overhaul, and the home reflects a modern sensibility with clean lines, minimal clutter, and nothing overtly feminine or masculine.

TO CREATE A COHESIVE LOOK in the open living-kitchen-dining area, paint colors draw from a palette of subtle blues and creams. Upholstered furniture and window treatments repeat the color scheme. Dark wood floors stretch from room to room with rugs defining lounging and dining areas.

FOR PERSONALITY, the homeowners opted for shapely pieces, such as a stacked bookcase and large lidded baskets. A few splurges, such as the dining room table, lighting (chandeliers, pendants, lamps), and the master bedroom headboard, display iconic modern design. Patterns on pottery, pillows, and artwork add just enough liveliness to keep the mostly neutral house from looking bland.

MODERN FURNISHINGS are small in scale or leggy to minimize visual weight and allow the house to live larger than its 1,800 square feet. A new sliding glass door and deck off the dining room extend living space into the treetops. Mirrors multiply views and light.

refresh
A stack of books with colorful covers creates a pillar of modern art.

before

SPARE SPACE

above **Contemporary furnishings that show a little leg keep the snug living room from seeming claustrophobic. Rugs rather than walls separate the living and dining rooms. The neutral palette provides visual resting spots.**

WELCOME HOME

opposite **A short hallway leading from the front door left zero space for an entry console. The solution? Extend the welcome into the living area with a roomy console and covered baskets, perfect for storage (this one holds shoes).**

refresh
A mirror hung above a wide console creates an entry along a spare wall.

modern tricks

Mix it up: Add interest and warmth to a modern space by combining opposites. Here, a rustic mirror pairs with a streamlined console.

Inject color: Neutrals ground a contemporary space while punches of color in accessories add a lively note.

Update classics: Traditional shapes and finishes, such as these metallic, urn-style lamp bases, expand the definition of contemporary.

LIGHT SHOW
Small-scale furniture and chairs you can see through make the dining room appear much bigger than it is. A wide curtain rod mounted above the sliding glass doors allows for maximum light when the panels are pushed back. A tray-top table serves as a mini bar.

refresh
A patterned bowl filled with fruit offers a variation on the standard bouquet.

before

KITCHEN TALK

above left **An** asymmetrical slab of walnut fastened to the half-wall outside the small kitchen creates a bar and breakfast spot that keeps everyone out of the cook's path. Blackboard paint turns a slice of wall into a convenient memo board.

DECKED OUT

top right **A new deck** off the dining room extends living space on the upper floor of the house. Outdoor furniture with modern shapes continues the style of the interior. One bright blue table breaks up the neutral scheme.

BEDROOM BLUES

above right **A massive** headboard adds structural interest to an otherwise ordinary bedroom and imparts a sense of enclosure. Layers of bedding, curtain panels, and wall paint—all in shades of blue—deliver a restful atmosphere.

refresh
A collection of white pottery makes a vintage cabinet look more modern.

CLASSIC CASUAL
This eating area links the kitchen's modern elements with the home's traditional detailing. Painting Queen Anne chairs black updates their classic silhouette without making them feel too modern.

before

fresh mix

Unexpected color combinations, bold patterns, and surprising furniture pairings saturate this classic New England home with look-at-me style.

What They Did. This house once had hunter green and burgundy walls with dated lattice carpet, a look the owners describe as more country club than Cape Cod. All that disappeared in a whirlwind four-week makeover that included hanging wallpaper, updating the kitchen and bathrooms, and installing a home office. Oh, and decorating changes were made to every room in the house.

TO WRITE THEIR COLOR STORY, these homeowners avoided the predictable in favor of hues they describe as mismatched. Shades of green and brown infuse all the rooms and unify the whole house scheme. Go-with colors include warm red, magenta, and golden yellow, plus unexpected pops here and there of electric blue or acid green pulled from a prized painting.

UPDATING TRADITIONAL STYLE, their design choices lean toward eclectic. Asian-style furnishings cozy up with modern as well as classic pieces. The turned legs of a Queen Anne chair contrast with the angular mass of a contemporary dining table. Light fixtures range from industrial pendants to a curvy chandelier.

DETAILS MATTER when you want family-friendly. Sink-in chairs in the family office invite long talks, the coffee table is large enough to put up your feet or assemble a puzzle, and plump pillows and textured upholstery add comfort.

refresh
Protect an accent table with a tray that keeps potential spills away from the table's surface.

TOUCHABLE TEXTURES
Texture plays a supporting role to pattern. Tell a story by combining opposites: a rattan-wrapped tray with a sleek ceramic vase or a soft chenille chair fabric with a smooth wood accent table. For continuity, repeat similar textures around the room.

SURFACE PLAY

right Every surface in a room is a place to introduce pattern, from a ceiling to pillows. Balancing their effect requires imagination and experimentation. Here, bold prints on the curtain panels and oversize pillows are weighed against the chairs' smaller motif and the stone grid of the fireplace.

GREENS TO ENVY

below A thread of green runs throughout the house, subtly tying the spaces together. In the dining room, the boldly patterned chartreuse wallpaper takes center stage. Geometric fabric on the chairs contrasts with the rambling wallpaper pattern.

before

mix not match

Get inspired: Use cherished pieces of art to inspire a color scheme. Add an unrelated pop of color as an unpredictable curiosity.

Facelift furniture: Mix styles and genres, such as upholstering clubby English chairs in a green-spotted ocelot pattern.

Think eclectic: Hang a delicate chandelier above a modern wood table or pair rattan blinds with a gilded mirror.

SUBTLE SMARTS
Instead of a total makeover, the homeowners updated the cabinets with subtle antiquing that highlights the recessed door panels. A new backsplash in oversize subway tiles and industrial-style lighting above the island inject a modern attitude.

before

refresh

Enliven a room with artwork in a hue that complements the furnishings.

SUPER OFFICE

right What more could you want in a home office than a treetop view, ample desktop space, built-in storage, and a soft comfortable chair? Acid green, daffodil yellow, and hot pink punctuate this room with energy.

PINK POWER

below A heady mix of patterns—from giant gingham and multicolor zigzag to damask—prevent this pink bedroom from feeling too sweet. Neutral walls put the bed in the spotlight.

when mixing patterns, think 60 percent of one pattern, 30 percent of a coordinating pattern, and 10 percent of an accent. Use a range of scales: for example, a narrow stripe, midsize geometric, and bold floral.

SW 6781
Jamaica Bay

SW 6782
Cruising

Nautilus

make it yours

Learn the skills needed to begin transforming your home today, from step-by-step solutions for problem areas to fun "make-it-better" projects.

step-by-step | *dressing the bed*

Outfit your bed in personal, stylish comfort by following these easy steps.

before

step 1

Give a neutral upholstered (or wood) headboard easy-change personality by draping a colorful throw over the frame. Stripes of grosgrain ribbon tie around the headboard for stability and appeal.

step 2

Cozy up the bed with a comforter that offers warmth and color.

step 3

Stack pillows for reading in bed. Use ones with varied thickness for flexible comfort. Mix and match pillowcases and shams; purchase extra pairs to change the look.

step 4

A plump throw pillow, the inspiration for the bedroom's palette, adds color and pattern. The shape of the pillow should contrast with the shams. Five pillows is the maximum most experts recommend.

F.Y.I.

Fold a colorful duvet across the foot of the bed. Sweet dreams!

SIDE NOTES
Dress up the nightstand with a lamp and accessories in complementary colors to give the room a finished look.

step-by-step | styling a buffet

Start with a basic piece of furniture, such as a bookcase, and turn it into a handsome sideboard for entertaining.

before:

step 1

Above a long, low piece of furniture, add vertical interest with a plywood panel covered in wallpaper and a striking starburst mirror.

step 2

Baskets in the cubbies work as open but portable drawers to hold small gear. Display pretty accessories on the counter.

step 3

Keep dishes and bowls handy for entertaining by stacking them in the other cubbies.

step 4

Skirt the bookcase. Cut a curtain panel in half, fold over the cut edges, and press. Attach ribbon to the panel using fusible tape. Place the curtain panel's pressed edges along the buffet's top edge, pleating the corners and overlapping the panels in the center; secure with decorative upholstery tacks.

EVERYDAY ELEGANCE
Whlle this project is geared to parties, a buffet will grace your home every day. Choose fabrics and accessories suited to the room so the piece fits right in.

F.Y.I.
Stage an appetizer party on plates and in elegant bowls and containers.

step-by-step | bookcase

Don't let your bookcase be a footnote to a room's decor. Give it an organized look and stylish personality.

before

Step 1

Using removable, double-stick tape, attach decorative paper to the cabinet back for added color and to offset books and objects.

Step 2

Organize books by subject, size, or color. Group books vertically on each shelf—for balance, position a wide group of books on opposite sides of adjacent shelves. Leave open at least a quarter of each shelf.

Step 3

Think of the bookcase as a shadow box. Add horizontal stacks of books to add variety and act as platforms for vases and small containers. Tuck in objects of similar shapes or finishes; slide art behind stacks for depth. Hang plates on the nearby wall to add presence.

Step 4

Conceal magazines or DVDs in deep, easy-to-reach baskets for a tidy look.

SKY LEVEL
Top a freestanding bookcase with groups of related objects in striking shapes to fill in the empty overhead space.

F.Y.I.
Take a step back to assess the overall balance of your arrangement often.

step-by-step | *coffee table*

Perk up your coffee table with an artful arrangement of favorite collected items.

 *before*

Step 1

Lay down a patterned area rug under the coffee table and sofa to define your room's seating area.

Step 2

Punctuate the tabletop with tidy stacks of items in a similar shape, size, and height. Include picture books to entertain guests. Add a vivid tray for a shot of color and to keep small items from straying. Square trays look best on circular tables.

Step 3

Place a shapely vase that's pretty enough to be displayed without flowers in the tray. Have votives and matches on hand for nighttime entertaining.

Step 4

Crown book stacks with a figurine or nut dish. Include a compote or open container to use as home base for electronics remotes.

FINISHING TOUCHES
Leave room on the tabletop for beverages or snacks. Reward your hard work and fill the vase with fresh flowers.

F.Y.I.
A coffee table should be no more than two-thirds of your sofa's total length.

step-by-step | *fireplace*

Rekindle a fireplace mantel's look and impact with lighting and accessories.

before:

step 1

Create a focal point: Position an attention-grabbing work of art in the center of the mantel. Pair a modern work of art with a traditional mantel to update classic decor.

step 2

Flank the art with a pair of lamps for symmetry and to cast a soft, candle-like glow. Lamps are an easy stand-in for hardwired sconces, and they lend a sculptural touch.

step 3

Use your mantel as a curio ledge and cluster decorative objects with similar, striking shapes. The brass urns mimic the lamps' curves.

step 4

Balance a group of large objects with a scattering of a few low items such as these bird figurines. Overlap pieces for a relaxed display. An unframed painting lends a quirky touch.

F.Y.I.

Create display platforms out of books to shift the mantel's landscape.

CHANGE-UP ARTIST

Mantels are the perfect place to display seasonal style and try out new ideas. Freshen up a room by changing the mantel display frequently.

EDWARD WESTON

[un]FASHION

the gastronomics reader

FASHION

BLOOM

step-by-step | art wall

Is the need to fill the empty wall above your sofa hanging over your head? Relax and follow a gallery-style approach to displaying art.

before

Step 1

Gather art or objects; select pieces with shared colors. Unify mismatched frames by painting them one color. Create paper patterns of the art. Tape patterns to the wall to test the display before you hang the pieces.

Step 2

Position the most prominent piece first, in the center at eye level. As you add pieces, keep the display's borders within the sofa's arms. Install picture-hanging hardware through the paper and then tear the paper away.

Step 3

Hang the next-largest pieces, aiming for balance. Sit one frame above the center art, the other at its side, for example. Keep the distance between all items uniform.

Step 4

Place pairs of plates or similarly sized art on both sides of the display for balance. Plates add shape and dimension too.

CLOSE THE GAP
Fill open areas with small works of like sizes and shapes until you're pleased with the symmetry. Play with orientation: Turn a square on end into a diamond, for example.

F.Y.I.
Don't forget the sofa—add pillows that pick up colors or patterns from your art.

buy it, make it better | *new*

Stack clay pots to create fun patio accessories.

before

step 1

Make end tables and planter pedestals by stacking various sizes of saucers and pots in creative combinations. Once you have the necessary pieces, assemble them without gluing first to make sure the result is what you envisioned.

step 2

Use a clear crafts adhesive to attach pieces, running a solid bead on each surface to be glued (a). Press pieces together. Let assembly dry. Spray on a coat of clay pot sealer to help the terra-cotta resist weathering.

Turn home-center items and laminated fabric into a party station.

step 1

Turn three shelves into a handy beverage depot. The top two shelves feature easy-to-install slotted molding for stemware.

step 2

To attach the molding, place the first piece about 1 inch from the inside edge of the shelf bracket; screw in place (a). Place the wineglass on the shelf board and position the next slat (b), leaving space so you can remove the stemware; screw in place. Add remaining molding, then hang shelves.

step 3

The bottom shelf is set on sturdy metal brackets and functions as a food prep table. Laminated fabric tacked to the shelf edge creates hidden storage.

F.Y.I.

Most home centers offer two free in-store cuts to lumber.

buy it, make it better | *new*

Secure a countertop to a pair
of bookcases to add function.

step 1

To create a counter-
height eating bar,
shop for 36-inch-high
bookshelves and a
countertop piece
that's 2 inches wider
than the shelves.

step 2

Set the countertop
on the bookcases
overlapping 1 inch on
each side and one
end (a). Use L brackets
to secure the counter
to the bookcases
and place the non-
overlapping end flush
against the wall.

step 3

Outfit the wall with
storage rods and
buckets that are
perfect for holding
small supplies (b).

F.Y.I.

**Plywood coated
with blackboard
paint turns any
frame into a mini-
chalkboard.**

buy it, make it better | vintage

before

Rehab a light fixture with spray paint and new paper shades.

step 1

To spray-paint the chandelier frame, cover the electrical light parts with painter's tape. Hang the frame from a low tree branch. Protect against overspray. Apply several thin coats of paint.

step 2

To make the shade pattern, mark the starting point on the shade and on paper; pencil the outline as you roll the shade (a). Add ½ inch at each end of the pattern for overlap. Transfer the shade shape to decorative paper (b); cut out as many as needed. Wrap paper around the shades; glue the overlap.

F.Y.I.

A touch of a bold color looks sophisticated against a neutral background.

buy it, make it better | *vintage*

A TV cabinet destined for the trash is transformed into a mudroom coat locker.

before

flip-flops

soccer @ 4
pizza party
Friday @ 5:30

AMY
BEN

step 1

Remove doors to create open shelves. Replace beat-up backing with a new board and paint the unit. Hang a 1×4 inside and attach coat hooks to it (a). Add a boot tray to catch dirt.

step 2

Equip shelves with baskets for storing seasonal items such as scarves, flip-flops, and sports gear. Mark them with tags (b).

step 3

Transform a side wall into a message center with dry-erase paint. Hang a wall pocket file for important papers and attach a key rack (c).

buy it, make it better | *vintage*

before

Top an outdated table with layers of batting and fabric for a fun pouf.

step 1

Sand, clean, prime, and paint the table.

step 2

Cut ½-inch-thick plywood to measure ½ inch smaller on all sides than the tabletop.

step 3

Cut four layers of batting to match plywood top. Cut a fifth layer of batting and one of fabric, both 3 inches wider on all sides than the plywood. Stack four batting layers on the fifth; center plywood on top. Pull batting around the plywood; staple on back. Repeat with fabric layer (a). Place cushion on table; screw through underside of table to attach pouf.

F.Y.I.

Glossy paint gives tired hardware a fresh look.

buy it, make it better | *vintage*

Old desks are cheap and plentiful;
revamp one to aid entertaining.

step 1

Shop for a desk slim
enough to fit in your
kitchen, sturdy
enough to glide on
casters, and with
multiple drawers.

step 2

Scrape off loose
paint, sand for a
smooth finish, and
prime. Paint the desk,
using a mohair paint
roller to achieve a
smooth finish.

step 3

Create movable
convenience by
installing casters and
then ready-made
ventilated shelves
(made for closets), cut
to length. The shelves
fill the desk's knee
space with slotted
wine storage ⓐ.
Store wine glasses in
file drawer.

F.Y.I.

**Elevate your
cutting board by
attaching wood
knobs to the
bottom.**

buy it, make it better | *vintage*

Turn vintage yardsticks into a dramatic and rustic mirror.

step 1

Cut a 36-inch circle from paper. Fold the paper in half, then in half again three more times to create 16 equally spaced creases in the circle.

step 2

Unfold the circle; center the mirror on it, trace around it, and remove. Cut yardsticks various lengths, allowing an extra 1 inch for assembling.

step 3

Arrange yardsticks on the circle, four or five per section; overlap at center by 1 inch (a). Stack and glue yardsticks to create irregular rays; let dry. Glue yardstick assemblage to the mirror's back (a).

F.Y.I.

Substitute paint stir sticks, dowels, or drumsticks for yardstick rays.

buy it, make it better | *vintage*

Rusty toolboxes clean up nicely to organize gear.

before:

step 1

Sand the box for a smooth finish, and prime with a rust-resistant paint. Paint inside and out with a metallic paint to ensure clean surfaces for storing gear.

step 2

Add glamour by lining interior compartments with art paper; attach using spray adhesive. Fill the box, taking advantage of the metal; use magnets to turn the lid into a memo board (a).

step 3

When not in use, the boxes can perch on metal brackets painted in a metallic finish.

F.Y.I.
Line drawers with silver-cloth fabric to prevent tarnish on silver items.

(a)

buy it, make it better | vintage

before

Rethink function and turn an old piece of furniture into a great kitchen cart.

step 1

Shop for furniture with an eye on rehabbing and repurposing. An old carpenter's bench works well as a kitchen cart. (If an old piece is painted, test it for lead before you use it near food.)

step 2

Removing a horizontal drawer support made room for a wire basket. The board now serves as a vertical divider in the adjacent niche.

step 3

Gently rehab the finish by scrubbing the workbench with hot water and oil soap that gently cleans wood. If the finish is too worn, wipe the surface with a nontoxic oil that's safe for use on surfaces that come in contact with food.

F.Y.I.

Attach locking casters to raise the bench height to 36 inches.

create | decoupage a chair

Revamp furniture with a paper
finish that's part art and totally fun.

F.Y.I.
To use newsprint
or any thin paper,
make a laser copy
(ink-jet copies
run in water).

step 1

Start with a clean piece of
furniture with a smooth
finish. Trace the shape of
the furniture piece onto
plain paper to create a
template. Place the template
on the image (a poster, in
this case) and move it
around to find and position
the section you want to use.
Using a pencil, lightly trace
the shape of the template
onto the image.

step 2

Following your tracing, cut
out the image (a) using
sharp scissors. It's better to
err on the side of too much
image—overlap is easily
trimmed using a very sharp
crafts knife. To adhere the
paper to the furniture, coat
the furniture surface with
decoupage medium, keeping
it wet until the paper is in
place. Dip the paper in a
tub of water (b) for about
10 seconds before placing.

step 3

Align paper with furniture
edges. Keep your hands wet
to prevent tearing. Use a wet
sponge or wet brayer to
work out excess decoupage
medium, water, and air,
moving hands and tools
outward from the center to
flatten the image onto the
surface. Let dry overnight.
Using a foam brush, seal the
surface with three to five
coats (one per hour) of low-
luster acrylic polyurethane.

create | make a wallpaper patchwork

Get scrappy and turn wallpaper remnants into a custom wall treatment.

step 1

A roll or two of wallpaper provides the background for this wall project. To find smaller blocks of wallpaper, try these affordable sources: closeout papers, returned rolls, samples (available for a small fee), and out-of-date wallpaper books. A wallpaper collection offers coordinating patterns designed to go together.

step 2

Using a mix of patterns—from small- to large-scale—cut wallpaper (a) into blocks of various sizes. A metal ruler or T-square, crafts knife, and self-healing mat (b) will help you make even cuts. There's no need to measure, but make sure the edges are square.

Step 3

Use wallpaper adhesive for the paste; it's surprisingly forgiving. You'll have about an hour to reposition papers before the glue dries. Paste large wallpaper sections on a wall, adjoining the edges; let dry. Paste smaller blocks over the base design, overlapping for a patchwork effect. Continue positioning blocks until you're satisfied with the look.

F.Y.I.

Stay within a set palette but mix pattern and scale with abandon.

create | paint on a memo board

Organize your work week in style with a six-pane window sash and specialty paints.

step 1

Purchase a single six-pane window sash to make a five-days-plus-notes memo board. You'll find windows in a variety of sizes at secondhand stores specializing in building supplies, such as Habitat for Humanity's ReStore. Choose a window with unbroken panes that don't move in the frame. Sand and paint the frame the desired color.

step 2

For the panes, use painter's tape to protect the front of the frame and old paper to catch overspray on adjacent panes. Spray magnetic paint on "notes" pane (a), following instructions on the paint can; let dry. Paint all the panes, including the magnetic "notes" pane, with chalkboard paint. Use a small paintbrush for the edges. Switch to a small foam roller for the center of the panes (b) to get a smooth surface. Let dry. Use chalk to write the days of the week and notes on each pane and use magnetic holders for hanging items on the "notes" pane.

F.Y.I.

Chalkboard paint turns anything into a memo board—from walls to plates.

create | refinish a frame

Add patina to a decorative frame with layers of paint.

step 1

Purchase a mirror with a frame that has carvings and raised moldings that can be highlighted by this decorative finish. Lightly sand the surface. Wipe clean with tack cloth. Brush the entire frame with a coat of silver acrylic paint (a), making sure to cover all cracks and crevices. Let dry for three to four hours.

step 2

Apply a coat of pearlized white acrylic paint (available at crafts stores and home centers) on top of the silver coat, allowing some of the silver to show through the pearl finish. Let dry for three to four hours.

step 3

Brush on dark brown acrylic paint, working in 12-inch segments on the mirror frame. Use a dry, lint-free cotton cloth (b) to immediately rub off the brown paint. Leave enough brown paint to give the piece its patina. Repeat the technique on the rest of the frame, taking care to blend segments where they join. Let dry for three to four hours. Apply a coat of clear latex sealant to protect the finish. Let dry.

F.Y.I.

Maximize a mirror's gleam with reflections of glass and metal.

create | trim a wall

Add character to plain drywall with this grid built from stock lumber pieces.

step 1

Paint wall and molding pieces. Measure your wall and map out a grid using a pencil and a level (a). This wall features two rows of 12×21-inch rectangles set in 19×28-inch rectangles.

step 2

Using a nail gun or hammer, apply 1×3 molding on the horizontal lines, starting at the top of the wall. If the ceiling/wall seam is not level, set the molding as close to the ceiling as you can while still keeping it level. Cut 1×2s to length to fit the vertical lines; nail them to the wall (b). Butt joints make this easy.

step 3

Cut molding to make a second 12×21-inch rectangle inside each larger rectangle, mitering the corners. Before installing the molding, paint a white 12×21-inch rectangle in the center of each section. Nail bottom molding on first; add the sides and finish with the top piece (c). The installed molding will cover the painted edges.

F.Y.I.

Use a miter box and saw to create perfect mitered corners.

create | redo a cupboard

before

a

b

F.Y.I.

Hooks attached to the sides of cabinets boost storage space.

Personalize a plain box of a cupboard using standard building materials.

step 1

Add design oomph with paintable wood details from a home center or crafts store. A simple change in orientation turns square rosettes into diamonds. Rope trim defines the door panels; layers of trim accent the top and bottom of the cabinet. Use wood glue and/or nails to secure all the pieces in place.

step 2

Recessed panels get a little more attitude with a frame of wood trim. Use slim pieces of molding; cut the ends at 90-degree angles (a) with a miter saw and miter box. Attach molding using wood glue.

step 3

Call attention to the wood embellishments with a fun paint finish. Sand and prime the cabinet. Apply a coat of semigloss paint as an undercoating for a decorative glaze; the glaze will slide more easily over the semigloss paint than over matte paint. Use a rag (b) to rub the decorative glaze over the entire cabinet; follow the manufacturer's directions for best results. Apply extra glaze to corners and decorative pieces.

create | fashion a planter

A can of spray paint, a vintage lamp, and vining plants combine to make magic.

F.Y.I.
Use farm and implement paint for a high-gloss surface and weather-resistant finish.

step 1
Choose a lamp base with an appealing shape and select a planting basket. Remove the shade and use wire cutters to remove the cord and other visible wiring. Prepare the base for paint by rubbing the surface with steel wool (a). Spray-paint base with primer; let dry.

step 2
Spray the lamp base with an outdoor paint (b). Follow the manufacturer's instructions for best results. Spray-paint the basket the same color. Allow both to dry completely.

step 3
Attach the basket to the lamp base using copper wire and pliers (c). If the base has no holes to use, drill four holes evenly spaced around the lamp top. Line the basket with a 1-inch layer of sphagnum moss to hold the soil. Vining plants, such as petunias, are a good choice

for cascading over the edges and covering the basket. For a striking foliage-only plant, use ivy. Be sure to water your planter often, as water evaporates quickly in open baskets such as this one.

Follow these simple techniques to paint stripes with absolutely crisp edges.

step 1

For this headboard, paint the base color on three 20×80-inch hollow-core doors; let dry. To create multiple stripes, plan a pattern that makes use of the base color and layer on other stripe colors.

step 2

For each stripe, use a level and a pencil (a) to lightly mark the top and bottom. Apply painter's tape just outside the pencil lines. Run a fingernail or credit card along the tape for a tight bond. Brush clear glazing liquid in matte finish (b) over the tape edges for a tight seal.

step 3

Let the glaze dry to the touch (30 to 60 minutes) and then roll on the paint. Make sure you roll over (but not past) the tape (c). Let dry for about an hour. Peel off the tape (d) to reveal the stripes. The glaze prevents any paint from working its way under the tape. Repeat steps 2 and 3, following your pattern.

(a)

(b)

(c)

(d)

create | build a headboard

A slipcovered headboard is the focal point of a bedroom and a personal design statement.

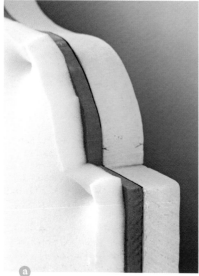

F.Y.I.

Play with pattern placement before you cut the headboard fabric.

step 1

Draw the size and shape for your headboard on paper. Cut the shape from ½-inch plywood using a jigsaw. Cut additional layers: one of insulating foam and one or two of foam or fabric batting. Glue the insulating foam to the back of the plywood to add visual heft with little weight. Staple foam or fabric batting to the front for a soft, cushioned surface (a).

step 2

Following the pattern, cut two pieces of decorator fabric, adding ½-inch seam allowances on all sides. Cut a long piece of fabric the thickness of the headboard, plus 1-inch seam allowances. For details on making piping and more on making the slipcover, go to *BHG.com/MakeoversHeadboard*. Sew the front, back, and gusset pieces together (b).

step 3

With a utility knife, carve out two small foam rectangles (c) for access to secure the bolts firmly to the headboard and bed. Cut two holes in the headboard slipcover to match the foam rectangles; hand-tack the raw edges to the inside. With the insulating foam facing the wall, bolt the headboard to the bed frame.

create | upholster a headboard

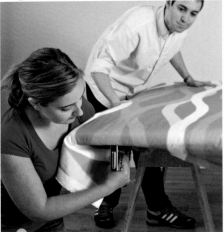

A pair of 32-inch-wide hollow-core doors provide the structure for this queen-size headboard.

step 1

Mark cut lines on each door panel . Saw to desired size. Line up sawed-off doors, noting location of interior wood framing. Link the doors by driving six to eight screws through furring strips into wood framing along the bottom edges. Repeat along headboard's top edge.

step 2

Cut fabric and batting 10–14 inches longer than the headboard's width. Spray upper portion of the headboard with adhesive (lower portion of headboard will not be upholstered: the bed will hide the wood). Line up the batting over the headboard and press into position. Spray on more adhesive and lay on second layer of batting. Lay fabric on top and straighten.

step 3

Working with a partner, smooth fabric and stretch it tight. Tack fabric and batting (c) in a few spots on the back with a staple gun.

step 4

Place the headboard face down and staple fabric and batting every 3 inches on the back. At corners , remove excess batting. Fold fabric as if wrapping a package and staple in place.

F.Y.I.

An electric staple gun simplifies this project and tightly secures the fabric.

create | add bath decals

Decorating possibilities abound with water-resistant peel-and-stick products in the bathroom.

(a)

(b)

step 1

Choose a decal pattern with colors and styles that will work in your bath. A variety of manufacturers offer peel-and-stick options. Select products with easy installation and a style you can personalize.

step 2

Striped borders highlight architectural details. For sharp corners and well-matched lines, look for a product that allows you to reposition to perfection. For example, this product features a removable and reusable static adhesive that lets you move it to a new location (a) by carefully peeling the product away from the glass surface.

step 3

Frosted adhesive film (b) **on this bathroom window makes for pretty privacy.** To apply, spray the window and back of the film with water; "float" the film into place.

F.Y.I.

Adhere decals to smooth surfaces such as glass, plastic, and finished wood.

Easy on and easy off, decals are perfect for the decorator with ever-changing tastes.

For a movable feast of wall art, create decals using sign-maker's vinyl. Scan, enlarge, and print out the outline of your flatware. Lay that pattern over the vinyl and use a sharp crafts knife to cut out the pieces and apply to plain plates (a). Light up a room by applying decals to a white lampshade and attach a pretty trim to the edges with hot glue (b). A horizontal pattern such as this alphabet (c) creates the look of a shelf to link a wall of hooks in an entry. Change the look of your dining room with seasonal, removable decals on the chairs (d).

create | stencil a wall

A large-scale stencil transforms a wall
with shapes and colors.

step 1

Paint the wall and allow it to
dry completely. Photocopy
your stencil and place the
copies on the wall to
determine your design's
placement. For a two-layer
stencil, start by spraying
stencil adhesive to the
back of the first stencil
and gently smooth it (a) to
the wall.

step 2

To paint a large stencil, use
a mini roller. A thin layer of
paint won't seep under the
edges of the design, so be
careful not to overload the
roller. Wipe off excess paint
with paper towels. Use light
pressure to roll paint over
the entire pattern (b) and
allow to dry.

step 3

For the second layer of the
design, spray the back of the
second stencil and line it up
carefully over the first
painted layer. Press to apply
stencil (c) to the wall.

step 4

Repeat step 2 in a second
color (d) to create depth in
your design.

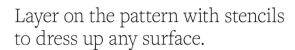

create | have fun with stencils

F.Y.I.

Combine matte and gloss paints in the same color for a fun effect.

Layer on the pattern with stencils to dress up any surface.

An intricate, allover pattern creates the look of vintage wallpaper (a) but is customized to the space. Make a lacy reverse stencil using real lace. Pin doilies to a solid-color pillow (b) and spray with permanent fabric paint. Large-scale stencils such as this clock face (c) become focal points. Repeating a cottage-style pattern (d) up a flight of stairs creates the look of a runner. Once the paint has thoroughly dried, seal the stairs with clear polyurethane to keep the design from wearing off with use.

Our tips, paint pointers, and handy measurements can make your project a success.

Painting kitchen cabinets

With a good paint job, you can avoid the cost and mess of replacing old cabinets. It's a manageable do-it-yourself project if you're patient. Expect to spend three to seven days painting a medium-size kitchen.

Here's how to get the best results:

Choose wisely. Pick a paint and primer designed for the surface of your cabinets. Most paint companies offer products for wood, metal, even laminate.

Map the parts. Though time-consuming, it's best to remove cabinet doors, along with hinges and handles. Save yourself frustration by carefully labeling each piece with its position for easier reassembly.

Make a test run. Before you paint all your cabinets, try the new color on the backs of several cabinet doors; prop them in place to evaluate the look.

Go for pro help. Consider painting cabinet boxes yourself and sending the doors to a professional for a super-smooth finish.

Selecting area rugs

Consider these seating principles to get the rug size just right.

In a dining room, make sure the rug accentuates the shape of the dining table and the legs of all the seating pieces fit well within the rug when the chair is being used, not just when pushed in.

For a living room layout with the sofa against a wall, the rug should fit under the front legs of all the seating pieces.

For a floating living room layout, make sure all seating legs fit on the rug.

24 inches is the minimum amount an area rug should extend beyond a bed on each side.

2 to 5 feet is optimal space between chairs and sofas.

Using wall anchors

Learn how to guarantee that art you hang stays up.

Anchor Type	Uses	What to Know	Drilling Required?	Damage Left Behind
PLASTIC SCREW ANCHOR	Light to medium-weight objects, such as a toilet-paper holder. Load capacity is 15–24 pounds.	These ribbed anchors split apart when screws are driven into them, gripping the drywall; also available in metal.	Yes. Drill the hole, use a hammer to tap in the plastic anchor, and insert the screw.	A hole just smaller than the diameter of the plastic anchor. The threads of the anchor will bite into the edges of the hole.
SCREW-IN DRYWALL ANCHORS	Light to medium-weight objects, such as a curtain rod or a towel bar. Load capacity is 15–40 pounds.	Available in plastic and metal.	No. Tap in the anchor; insert the screw.	A hole just smaller than the diameter of the plastic anchor.
TOGGLE BOLTS	Medium-weight to heavy objects, such as a handrail or track lighting. Load capacity is 35–70 pounds.	Anchors expand two wings behind the drywall. When the anchor is removed, the wings drop into the wall cavity.	Yes. Drill the hole, insert the folded anchor, and turn the screw to tighten.	A hole just large enough to fit the closed toggles through.

5 painter's must-haves
The right tools make a project easier and the results more professional.

Sanding blocks make for quick, easy work and yield a smooth finish.

A 2½-inch tapered brush is perfect for painting trim and cutting in corners. Quality, natural-bristle brushes work well with latex paint.

Mohair paint rollers create a flawless finish perfect for doors, cabinets, and trim.

Xylol-base primer covers even shiny paneling, and priming is key to painting over dark wood. It has a strong odor, so keep the work area well ventilated.

High-quality acrylic latex paint covers just as well as oil-base formulas but uses fewer toxic chemicals, dries quicker, is easier to clean, and won't yellow.

Beddy buys
Know your numbers before you start shopping.

Replace your mattresses every eight to 10 years.

Consider basic bed measurements before you go shopping and add 4 to 12 inches at each end for a headboard and footboard. Bed coverings such as blankets and duvets add about 3 inches to both sides of the bed. If possible, allow 24 to 36 inches of clear space on the sides and at the foot of the bed.

Buy the right size.
Twin: 38/39×75 inches
Extra-Long Twin: 38/39×80 inches
Double/Full Size: 54×75 inches
Queen: 60×80 inches
King: 76/78×80 inches
California King: 72×84 inches

Mattresses used to be a standard 9 inches thick. Today many manufacturers make "extra deep" mattresses as the norm. These styles, many of which are up to 16 inches thick, may or may not mean more comfort.

Check mattress construction. Compare the number of coils and their construction, the number of padding layers and their materials, and special features. The higher the number of coils, the better the bed will wear. A guideline is 300 coils for a double, 375 for a queen, and 450–600 for a king. Opt for ones topped with several layers of upholstery, one or more layers of foam, and a quilted pillow top.

Know your numbers

8 inches—This standard shelf depth is deep enough to provide display space.

4 to 5 feet—Allow this space for traffic flow into and through rooms—enough room for two people to pass each other.

2½ to 3 times—For luxurious fullness, buy curtains that measure more than double the window width.

3 feet and 6 feet—Ladder heights needed for most wall painting projects.

60-30-10—Perfect your decorating palette with 60 percent in the main color, 30 percent in the secondary color, and 10 percent for the accent.

5 gallon bucket—Size of container to use for mixing to assure a consistent color if you're using up to four gallons of the same tinted paint.

30 to 36 inches wide is the perfect size for a table to encourage conversation.

What month does it go on sale?

JANUARY
Carpet & flooring

MARCH, SEPTEMBER
China & flatware

MAY, JUNE, DECEMBER
Cookware

JANUARY, JULY, HOLIDAY WEEKENDS
Furniture

SUMMER
Mattresses
Paint

AFTER LABOR DAY
Patio furniture

DECEMBER
Small appliances

EARLY SPRING, ALSO SIX TO 12 MONTHS AFTER A PARTIUCLAR MODEL IS LAUNCHED
Televisions

Painting (almost) anything
Use this chart to find the best way to paint the surfaces in your home.

Product	Supplies	Preparation	Painting	Tips
BRICK	Wire brush, trisodium phosphate (TSP) cleaner or muriatic acid, white vinegar, baking soda, masonry sealer, latex paint	Scrub brick with TSP or muriatic acid. Rinse with vinegar, then rinse with 2 tablespoons baking soda per gallon of water.	Apply a masonry sealer, then use a long-nap foam roller to apply paint. Use a brush to get paint into the grout lines and crevices.	Wait 30 days before painting newly installed brick. Removing paint damages brick, so a change is permanent.
LAMINATE	Lacquer thinner, bonding primer, latex or plastic paint	Clean surface with a lacquer thinner. This will remove grease and oil and open up the pores of the laminate, making it receptive to paint.	Apply two thin coats of a bonding primer designed to increase the paint's adhesion to the slick, shiny surfaces.	Test products in a hidden area before painting the whole surface. That way, you can be certain you'll be happy with the results.
CERAMIC TILE	150-grit sandpaper, trisodium phosphate (TSP) cleaner, bonding primer or ceramic primer, gloss or semigloss latex or plastic paint	Sand tiles lightly to increase adhesion and wash the surface with TSP to remove dirt and grease.	Apply a bonding primer or a primer for ceramic or glass (found at crafts stores). Use latex paint or paint suited for shiny plastics.	For best coverage, paint the grout too.
PLASTIC	150-grit sandpaper, trisodium phosphate (TSP) cleaner, spray paint for plastic	Sand surface lightly to increase adhesion. Wash with TSP; be careful not to touch the surface after cleaning (you can leave oil from your skin).	Use a spray paint designed for plastic, following the instructions on the label. Use multiple thin coats for best coverage.	When using spray paint, hold the can 10–12 inches away from the surface. If it's too close, you'll have drips; too far, uneven coverage.
METAL	Wire brush, 150-grit sandpaper, rag, spray primer, spray paint for metal	Use the wire brush to remove flaking paint. Sand the surface to help the paint adhere. Wipe the item with a damp rag and let it dry.	Apply a primer and paint for metal. The paint should include corrosion inhibitors to help prevent rust.	For weather-worn metal pieces, apply rusty-metal primer to prevent additional deterioration of the surface.
WOOD	Rubbing alcohol, scouring pad, sponge, 150-grit sandpaper, lightweight surfacing compound, oil-base sealer, oil-base or latex paint	Scour with rubbing alcohol and rinse with water and a sponge. Sand rough areas and wipe away dust. Fill holes with surfacing compound.	Apply two coats of sealer and two coats of paint. Use a roller to apply paint, but use a brush to finish the surface with smooth strokes.	Avoid bargain paint. Higher-quality paints have more pigments and binders, so you need fewer coats.
CONCRETE	Trisodium phosphate (TSP) cleaner, bleach solution, degreasing solution, concrete patch, muriatic acid, hydrodynamic sealer, masonry paint	Clean with TSP, then bleach solution. Degrease oily spots. Repair cracks. Etch surface with 10% solution of muriatic acid and water.	Apply a hydrodynamic sealer and two or three coats of paint specifically designed for concrete floors.	An epoxy paint is impervious to oil and stains, making it a good choice for garage floors.
DRYWALL	Dust mop, trisodium phosphate (TSP) cleaner, lightweight surfacing compound, wallboard sealer or stain-blocking primer, latex paint	Dust walls with a clean mop and wash them with TSP. Scrape off loose paint and fill any holes with surfacing compound.	For new drywall, use a wallboard sealer. For existing drywall, use a stain-blocking primer to help hide water stains. Apply two coats of paint.	Make sure you have enough paint on the roller, but not an excessive amount. If you apply too much paint, it will start to sag on the wall.

Working with paint chips

Paint-chip cards provide a look at tints and shades to help organize paint collections from a single manufacturer.

Value is the lightness or darkness of a color. Paint-chip cards typically have light and dark variations of one color. Sky blue is a light value; cobalt is a dark value. Use light yellow in one room, for example, and a deeper hue from the same paint-chip card in an adjoining room. For delineation, pick colors separated by at least one chip on a card.

Shades are colors that have been dulled with black or gray. Shades can be near the top of the paint-chip card or at the bottom.

Intensity refers to color saturation and specifies clearness or brightness. Adding white, black, or a complementary color to a pure color diminishes its intensity. To ensure the same intensity for contrasting colors, select hues from the same position on the paint-chip cards, using the same brand.

Tints, often called pastels, are closest to white in value. You'll find them on the top of a paint-chip card or in a separate collection of whites and off-whites. Tints can appear almost white or stronger in hue.

Office basics

Desktop. Plan a desk height of 26 inches for a computer keyboard and 30 inches for a crafting table. If you have room for only one work surface, install the desktop at the higher measurement and add a pullout keyboard shelf beneath it.

Storage. Standard filing cabinets provide efficient storage. Use a closet with pullout bins to organize bulky supplies. Gain more hidden storage by skirting the desk and a few bookcases.

TV to-dos

Shop for a new flat-panel television with these tips in mind.

Mark the spot. Determine eye-level placement of your TV by sitting in the prime viewing spot or lying in bed. Have a helper mark the TV outline on the wall using painter's tape. The middle of the TV should be close to eye level.

Measure the distance. A long-standing rule is that the best viewing distance is twice the screen's diagonal measurement. But with improved technology, you can sit farther away. At home, measure the distance from the TV to your viewing spot; view from that distance in the store to assess the picture's quality.

Get the best angle. Straight-on viewing is ideal. But flat panels, especially plasma TVs, have a wide viewing angle, so side viewing is less compromised.

36 square feet is the area covered by a single roll of wallpaper. Most wallpaper, however, is sold in double rolls. Read labels carefully.

60–66 inches from the floor is eye level for hanging artwork.

Fine dining

When planning a dining room, take these factors into account.

A dining room often has to hold more furniture than recommended. Optimum clearance from table edge to the nearest wall or obstacle is 5½ feet. That means if your table is 6 feet long, the room should be about 17 feet long.

The table needs to allow elbowroom, about 30 inches between chair centers. But it shouldn't be too big for passing dishes comfortably.

Dining chairs, including arms, should fit under the table. Sit down and cross your legs to check that there is ample space between the table apron and your thighs.

The rug should extend at least 16 inches beyond all edges of the table and remain under chair legs even when people are seated.

Unless you have high ceilings and a chandelier positioned above head height, a chandelier should be at least 12 inches narrower than an oval or rectangular dining room table and 18 inches smaller than a round tabletop. Otherwise, people could bump their heads when standing up. Generally the bottom of your fixture should be about 30 to 36 inches above the tabletop.

Tabletop centerpieces should be about 16 inches tall. This allows your guests to see across the table. The place settings should be positioned side to side and across from each other with the arrangement between the diners.

Special thanks to:
*York Wallpaper, Dash
& Albert, Land of Nod,
and Paper Source for
providing materials used
in "Buy it, Make it Better."*

live with *style*

Look for budget-friendly home improvements, smart decorating ideas, and space-saving solutions in these new Better Homes and Gardens® books.

Better Homes and Gardens.

An Imprint of **HMH**

Better Homes **NEW DECORATING BOOK**

Better Homes and Gardens.
small bath solutions

Better Homes
COLOR
the complete guide for your home

• Paints
• Palettes
• Patterns

Better Homes and Gardens®
real-life decorating
Your Look, Your Budget

Better Homes and Gardens
storage WITH STYLE

Baths
Closets
Kitchens
Mudrooms
Home Offices

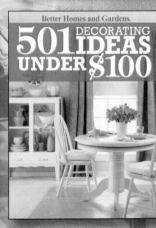

Better Homes and Gardens.
501 DECORATING IDEAS UNDER $100